Theology Today
2 Theology and Revelation

Nihil obstat:
Jeremiah J. O'Sullivan, D.D.
Censor deputatus
19th January 1968

Imprimatur:
† Cornelius Ep. Corcag. & Ross
25th January 1968

Cum licentia superiorum ordinis

ISBN 0-85342-159-5

Theology Today

GENERAL EDITOR:
EDWARD YARNOLD, S.J.

No. 2

Theology and Revelation

BY

GERALD O'COLLINS, S.J.
Pembroke College, Cambridge

distributed by
CLERGY BOOK SERVICE
BUTLER, WISCONSIN

ACKNOWLEDGEMENTS

The Scripture quotations in this publication are from the *Revised Standard Version of the Bible*, copyrighted 1946 and 1952 by the Division of Christian Education of the National Council of the Churches of Christ in the U.S.A. and used by kind permission· Quotations from *The Documents of Vatican II* (ed. W. M. Abbott, S. J.) are printed by kind permission of The America Press and Geoffrey Chapman Ltd., London.

ABBREVIATIONS

PG J. P. Migne: *Patrologia Graeca.*
PL J. P. Migne: *Patrologia Latina.*
Dz H. Denzinger & A. Schönmetzer,
     *Enchiridion Symbolorum, Definitionum
     et Declarationum* (33rd edit., Barcelona etc., 1965).

To M. P. and J. G.

CONTENTS

PREFACE

Christ is the subject of all theology. The first volume of this series was therefore a study of the Incarnation.

But how do we encounter Christ? Through revelation. For the revealing Word spoken to man by the Father is Christ.

The biblical enrichment of our theology, to which the Council gave such spectacular impetus, has disclosed area after area of Catholic teaching which is after all acceptable to those outside the Roman Church. In no field perhaps has this development been more marked than in the theology of revelation.

Fr. O'Collins has written just such a biblical theology of revelation finding in the Scriptures, which are the record of revelation, the clues to the understanding of what revelation is.

E. J. Yarnold, S. J.

INTRODUCTION

Christianity understands itself to be a revealed religion. Christians are convinced that God has made himself known in the Old and New Testaments, manifesting himself in Jesus of Nazareth as the loving Father who saves us. Yet – broadly speaking – it has only been in modern times that the nature of revelation has become a subject of general theological discussion. What had been quietly assumed or taken over as obvious by Christians was questioned and for various reasons rejected by such movements as deism, rationalism, pantheism, positivism and materialism. When this challenge to the implicit Christian consensus came, 'revelation' was made the theme of much theological writing. The debate was reflected in the two Vatican Councils which published explicit and reasonably lengthy statements on revelation.

A special difficulty in talking about revelation derives from the fact that it is the constant presupposition to all our talk about particular events or details of the Christian religion. In a sense our doctrine of revelation encloses and affects the whole of theology. With such expressions as 'the word of God', 'salvation history' and 'the divine promises' it is among the most general terms available, describing in principle and comprehensively the 'object' of faith and the 'content' of theology. To speak of revelation is in a way to speak of the whole of Christianity. Hence any systematic synthesis is difficult. We are dealing here with a living reality, the relations between God and man in Christ, which defy reduction to a series of neat formulae.

7

In a spirit of 'faith seeking understanding' we spend most of this book exploring revelation from various angles and conclude by outlining one particular theology of revelation.

Right from the outset one point should be made clear. Revelation is not primarily the disclosure of new truths about God, the communication of a body of doctrine, a broadening or enriching of our knowledge of God. It is rather the saving self-revelation of God who calls us in Jesus Christ to enter by faith into a new relationship with him. The Son of God become man reveals not a system to be understood, but a discipleship to follow. His 'truth' is not an object of intellectual reflection, but the way of life (Jn 14. 6).

It is true that many Catholic manuals and books of apologetics have talked of revelation as if it were identical with the communication of a set of divinely-authenticated truths or with the body of information itself thus communicated to man. Revelation tended to be thought of as correct doctrine or as a creed. Now we don't wish to dispute or deny that it makes sense to speak of the 'content' or the 'truths' of revelation. Ultimately, however, revelation does not mean a relation to things, but a personal meeting in man's history. It is within this context that our talk of 'revealed truths' can find its appropriate place.

In its statements on revelation Vatican I gives the impression of being over-intellectual. It seems to lay nothing else before us than a theology of revelation in which God imparts to man divinely authenticated truths. The faith which responds to this disclosure is described as an obedient acceptance of these revealed truths, 'a supernatural virtue by which we believe that the things which he has revealed are true' (Dz 3008). To our age which feels that it has recovered a proper sense of the personal the account of faith in Vatican II is more attractive. The intellectual acceptance is seen as part of man's total self-commitment to the self-revealing God. ' "The obedience of faith" (Rom 16. 26; cf. 1. 5; 2 Cor 10. 5-6) must be given to God who reveals, an obedience by which man entrusts his whole self freely to God, offering "the full submission of intellect and will to God who reveals", and freely assenting to the truth revealed by him' (*Constitution on Divine Revelation* 1. 5).

In the formulation of its teaching on divine revelation and faith Vatican I was clearly influenced by St Thomas Aquinas, the opening article of the *Summa Theologica* being used and echoed by the Council (cf. Dz 3005). St Thomas – if one agrees that Pierre Benoît has correctly interpreted him – has a propositional view of revelation, i.e. one which prefers to understand revelation as the communication of divine truths otherwise inaccessible to human reason. Now it is not that such a propositional view of revelation should be dismissed as wrong, but contemporary theology senses that is it not ultimate. The relationship of the revealing God and the believing man is a living experience which is part of man's personal history. This reality can, of course, be in some way expressed through propositions. Provided these statements give some insight into the living experience of revelation, they can be described as expressing revelation. In this way it would be fair to talk of revelation as propositional or – perhaps better – propositionable. The faith which arises in the encounter with the self-revealing God can articulate itself in statements of faith. It is not wholly incommunicable. It does not remain locked up in inarticulate subjectivity, but formulates its experience in a coherent account. At the same time, however, even if revelation can thus come to expression in doctrinal propositions, it is not in

9

the first instance a disclosure of new truths, a broadening of man's knowledge as it were. Ultimately it is better understood as an historical call in Christ to enter a personal relationship with God, a saving call which creates the possibility of this relationship.

After saying all this we must ask whether Vatican I leaves us with what is merely a propositional view of revelation? If the council fathers in fact failed to go to what we would consider a deeper level this would be excusable. While still retaining its truth every formula in which faith is expressed can in principle be surpassed. Statements about the infinite divine reality are never absolutely satisfying; there are no final formulations. Christian understanding remains in a state of consistent self-questioning and re-assessment. Have theologians today – or has Vatican II in its constitution on revelation – expressed something which was passed over or at least not stated explicitly in the earlier formulations? A Protestant theologian who has entered a plea in defence of Vatican I over this issue is Heinrich Ott, the successor of Karl Barth at Basel. In a study of the teaching of Vatican I he argues that this council held on to the notion of revelation as an event that is both personal and creative. He draws attention to such passages as that which speaks of 'God *revealing himself* and the eternal decrees of *his will*' (Dz 3004). The council explains further how this divine self-revelation took place in the person and history of Jesus of Nazareth; in the concrete that is what it meant for God to reveal himself. 'The eternal decrees of his will' are God's saving acts in the Old and New Testaments – acts which were fulfilled in Christ but which await their final consummation. In reflection on Heb 1. 1f. Vatican I thus describes revelation in terms of a personal self-disclosure in history. At the same time, however, such an appreciation is far more explicit and developed in the constitution on divine revelation from Vatican II. The relevant sections from this constitution are printed as an appendix to this book.

There is a particular reason why it seemed worthwhile to begin this study with some remarks about the relation between (a) the view of revelation as propositional and (b) the view of revelation as personal encounter with the self-revealing God. It has been reasonably common practice for writers to begin discussions of revelation by making a sharp distinction between these two views. Such treatments can easily ignore the fact that these explanations are concerned with different aspects and stages of God's self-communication to man. Moreover, it seems a fair guess that some writers will represent the development between the two Vatican Councils as a progression from view (a) to view (b). Such a claim needs the kind of qualifications that have been briefly indicated. After these preliminaries we can begin our investigation of revelation, starting from the biblical evidence.

CHAPTER 1

REVELATION IN ISRAEL

What is meant by revelation is expressed in the bible through a multiplicity of words and phrases. The terminology for revelation in scriptures is not systematic and is not met with as often as might be suggested by the frequency with which modern theologians speak of revelation. In fact it is hardly a common biblical term, and in the New Testament – as we shall see – is mainly reserved for the revelation to come at the end of time. Yet it is important to realize that it would be a narrow procedure to limit discussion to the explicit biblical terminology for revelation. The fact that something is not being said very often or is not being said in the words which we might expect does not mean that something is not going on. It would be trivial to consider merely the level of textual expression. One must refer back to the events and words of which the texts in question speak. St John's Gospel, e.g., does not talk of Christ as a divine revealer, but it clearly intends his words and actions to be understood as revelatory. The scriptures are more interested in the fact of revelation than in the notion of revelation or in formal reflection about it. What then does the biblical evidence suggest about the existence and structures of revelation?

Revelation is commonly described as 'historical' and the Jewish-Christian religion as an historical religion. This means that the Jewish-Christian faith in a self-revealing God focuses its attention on particular localities and particular periods of time – on what happened to Abraham, Isaac and Jacob, on an exodus from Egypt and a covenant made on Mount Sinai. Through the course of human history God is revealed in that datable, localizable men encounter him in his self-disclosing activity. He is understood by his historical relations as the God of Abraham, Isaac and Jacob. His revelation has a 'there and then', a 'history' – at least on man's side. It is innerwordly and historical, for it comes at definite times and epochs to a definite set of people.

To speak of revelation as 'historical' involves too the claim that God acts in history; particular historical events are recognized as the means of divine self-disclosure. In the broadest sense revelation through the divine acts in history can cover a wide range of very different stories in which God is represented as acting and manifesting his intention: e.g. the creation, the flood, the exodus, the Babylonian captivity, the resurrection of Jesus and the destruction of Jerusalem. Then too the wisdom literature, e.g. the book of Proverbs, shows us men pondering on their lives as individuals and seeing there both the hand of God and the truth of human existence. The stories in which God is described as acting can concern whole groups – e.g. the human race in general and the people of Israel – or individuals such as the patriarchs of Israelite pre-history and the anonymous psalmists. In relation to the theme of revelation let us look at some of these stories in detail.

The 'primal history' (*Urgeschichte*) found in the first eleven chapters of Genesis is relatively late in composition, dating probably from the time of the Israelite kings and reflecting a situation of debate with contemporary myths and mythologies, especially the Babylonian. These chapters are drawn from various traditions and form a complex literary, prophetic and cultic document. What we learn there is how on the basis of the specific experience of God in her own history Israel thought about the origins of the world and the human race. These chapters give an answer to the question: What must the beginning have been like for the present to be what it is? From her living experience of human guilt, suffering and death Israel sought through theological reflection and divine illumination to understand her present situation and give an account of man before God. This theological description of man becomes a story projected on the screen of the past. Thus, e.g., the second account of creation (Gen 2. 4b-25) and the description of paradise (Gen 3) show man as the recipient of a gracious divine self-revelation and the object of God's intimate friendship and love.

In the story of her founding through Abraham and continuing life what Israel recognized as characteristic was not her own achievement but the history of divine salvation being progressively disclosed. The exodus and the occupation of Canaan were recalled as being not merely due to special divine intervention but also as clean contrary to human expectation. In all this Israel saw the hand of God as a guarantee and promise of what was to come; here was her ground for faith and hope. In this history Israel discerned the gracious will of Yahweh in her regard, a free choice which was not necessarily demanded either by the divine nature or by man's creation. Yahweh was the God of history, not some god of nature whose existence and action were characterized by necessity. In the fertility cults of the contemporary middle-eastern peoples the god of nature could be known in and through the seasonal cycle. The ritual myths of fertility saw the god dying at the end of each harvest time to be resurrected the following spring. For the Israelites, however, Yahweh was the lord of history We can cite the opening words of an ancient confession of faith.

And Joshua said to all the people, 'Thus says the

Lord, the God of Israel, "Your fathers lived of old beyond the Euphrates, Terah, the father of Abraham and of Nahor; and they served other gods. Then I took your father Abraham from beyond the River and led him through all the land of Canaan, and made his offspring many. I gave him Isaac; and to Isaac I gave Jacob and Esau. And I gave Esau the hill country of Seir to possess, but Jacob and his children went down to Egypt. And I sent Moses and Aaron, and I plagued Egypt with what I did in the midst of it; and afterwards I brought you out'" (Jos 24. 2-5).

Yet what right had Israel to understand a particular set of events as acts of God which revealed the divine intentions in her regard? How could the Israelites be justified in seeing the hand of God in certain observable episodes of their history, e.g. the conquest of Canaan? We are not requiring that they should have acted like impartial observers trying to see these events 'from the outside', as it were. No, they experienced and remembered these events 'from the inside'. The past was their own living and enduring past which had made them what they were. Pondering on the origin and purpose of their existence in terms of what happened in their national and individual history they saw a pattern in episodes which still retained reality for them in their contemporary world. In this history the intentions of Yahweh were revealed for them as the intentions of a personal agent in their regard. In making this judgment, however, did the Israelites have merely the events themselves to go on?

No, they were convinced that Yahweh had also revealed himself directly – in vision and word. This direct revelation removed the ambiguity which may otherwise have faced them in grasping the meaning of their history. The divine help was there to interpret what they experienced, ensuring that the events of their history were understood in terms of a personal relationship with Yahweh. Thus word (and vision) and event complemented one another in revelation. As Amos remarked, 'surely the Lord God does nothing, without revealing his secret to his servants the prophets' (3. 7). The divine word to the prophets (and others) and their proclamation of it preceded the coming events and took away from them the anonymity of meaningless strokes of fate. The events could be seen as Yahweh's doing and supremely personal in their intention. As Vatican II remarks:

> This plan of revelation is realized by deeds and words having an inner unity: the deeds wrought by God in the history of salvation manifest and confirm the teaching and realities signified by the words, while the words proclaim the deeds and clarify the mystery contained in them. (*Divine Revelation*, 1. 2).

Let us examine then the structures of direct revelation, or revelation by way of encounter if we prefer that expression. Then in terms of this direct revelation and the indirect revelation mediated by the events in history we can discuss some relevant questions about Old Testament covenant and prophets.

In the Old Testament God is often said to appear and to make himself known. The prophets are those who receive a vision; they are 'seers'. It would be a mistake to understand such visual expressions too literally. What is meant is some form of encounter with God. Benoît has rightly warned us to be cautious in interpreting such biblical talk as that of God 'appearing' to Abraham at Mamre (Gen 28. 1) and to Moses in the burning bush (Exod 3. 12). For God is also said to 'appear' by manifesting his glory (Is 40. 5; 60. 2), his justice (Is 56. 1) and his love (Ps 85. 8). God is described as 'showing himself a tower of strength' (Ps 48. 3). What is called a 'vision' can turn out to be merely the reception of a message. With 'eyes wide open' and 'penetrating gaze' Balaam sees a vision, but this means simply that God puts words into his mouth (Num 24. 15-16; cf. 22. 38; 23. 5, 16). Samuel's 'vision' consists in his hearing God's word; God is revealed in Samuel's call (1 Sam 3. 1, 4, 7, 10, 15, 17). In fact we can even read: 'The word seen by...' (Is 2. 1) or 'behold the word of Yahweh' (Jer 2. 31). At the same time it is true that some visions are represented as genuinely involving visual experience, e.g. those of Is 6. 1ff. and Ezek 1. 4ff. But in general 'to appear' and 'to be seen' mean that God has in some way disclosed himself and communicated a message, very often a promise. Thus 'the Lord appeared to Abram, and said, "To your descendants I will give this land"' (Gen 12. 7). We return later to the connection between revelation and promise.

Those who see 'visions' of God normally hear the word which clarifies the meaning of the appearance in question (cf. Is 6. 8; Ezek 2. 1; Jer 1. 11-14; Amos 7. 3; 8. 2ff.). Yet often there is only a hearing of the word; the whole revelation consists in that. The fact that God has spoken suggests the deeply personal nature of his revelation. It is perfectly true, of course, that man may speak to man in a thoroughly impersonal way, e.g. mechanically passing on information of a neutral kind. But God's word is never like that. It is a disclosure of the divine will which calls man to repentance and back into a relationship of obedience and love.

We should note, however, that we frequently find such formulae as 'The word of Yahweh was addressed to so and so in these terms' (e.g. 2 Sam 7. 4; 1 Kg 6. 11; 13. 20; 17. 2, 8; Jer 1. 4, 11). Many of the prophetic books begin 'The word of Yahweh that came to...'; thus Hosea, Micah, Joel, Zephaniah, and Malachi. This is the equivalent of the stereotyped expression 'The vision seen by...' (cf. Is 1. 1; Amos 1. 1; Nah 1. 1; Obad 1. 1). These stock phrases create a problem regarding the historical authenticity of the experience. We return to this shortly.

A high-point in direct revelation comes with the disclosure of the divine name to Moses, 'I am who I am' or 'I am what I am' or 'I will be what I will be' (Exod 3. 14). For the Semites there was, of course, a much closer bond between the name and the person than there is for contemporary western man. In a sense the name was identical with the person. Yet the revelation and explanation of the divine name of Yahweh falls short of being a manifestation of the divine essence. It is a call to acknowledge him as the one true God who controls the destiny of Israel. 'I am the Lord your God from the land of Egypt; you know no God but me, and besides me there is no saviour' (Hos 13. 4). The passage from Exod 3. 14 may reflect merely an attempt to understand the traditional but puzzling name 'Yahweh', the explanation being attributed to God himself.

Our discussion of 'visions', the word of God and the revelation of the divine name raises the obvious question about the Old Testament record. Can we know whether in fact some genuine revelatory encounter took place? In Hosea 'the Lord' may declare, 'I spoke to the prophets; it was I who multiplied visions' (12. 10), but not all that is presented as if it were a vision or a word from God can be accepted as such. As we have noted, the story in Exodus of the interpretation of the divine name given to Moses could be simply an explanation by later Israelites projected onto the screen of Moses' history. Sometimes it is clear that the biblical writers and the traditions they draw on attribute something to God to ensure authority for their statements.

19

Thus much detailed moral legislation in Leviticus is introduced by the rubric 'The Lord said to Moses'. Have we then any criteria by which to identify the material which could record genuine revelatory experiences of the Israelites? Firstly, we can exclude some passages on the grounds that the ascription of the material to God bears all the marks of being a conventional literary device. Where the style is seen to be that of contemporary formalized religious writing and the content is recognized to have parallels among the records of non-Israelite religious groups, we would easily tend to think of the material as part of the common religious patrimony of the ancient near East and not the product of a 'special' divine revelation to the Israelites. Other criteria could be the date, the nature and the number of the traditions recording some revelatory event. A single late account would obviously not carry the weight of several traditions that might be traced back close to the alleged event and testify to it in different ways perhaps with a certain allowable conflict of detail. Eventually such a process of discrimination would leave us with a number of incidents, e.g. divine encounters with such persons as Abraham, Moses and Isaiah. These episodes were remembered, recorded, and proclaimed in Israel, and helped to shape the Israelites' religious being and faith. The firm existence of these experiences in Israel's memory is clear. But what actually happened to give rise to the proclamation of these encounters with God remains problematical. Even if *per impossibile* the standard of the records was that of modern, scientific thoroughness, our judgment would obviously be affected by the fact that we accepted – or did not accept – the Jewish-Christian faith. To believe in Christ as *the* mediator of the divine self-disclosure involves us in holding that the Old Testament does record some previous revelation. Christ was born into a people about whom we say a number of things which imply divine revelation, e.g. that God had chosen this people and made a covenant with them. It is another and much more difficult thing to establish precisely how, when, where and to whom this revelation came.

At any rate by the close of the Old Testament we find among the Israelites such steadfast convictions as that Yahweh is the living God in an exclusive, incomparable sense: 'I am the Lord, and there is no other, besides me there is no God' (Is 45. 5; cf. Exod 20. 1-6). He is the personal creator who governs the world: 'I made the earth, and created man upon it; it was my hands that stretched out the heavens, and I commanded all their host' (Is 45. 12; cf. 48. 12-13 and Job 38-9). Yahweh is the holy one who calls man to a service of love (Lev 11. 44-45; 19. 2; 20. 7, 26; Hos 11. 1ff.), the master of history who guides events towards the goal of universal salvation: 'The Lord has bared his holy arm before the eyes of all the nations; and all the ends of the earth shall see the salvation of our God' (Is 52. 10). This is the Lord who chose the Israelites to be his people, brought them out of Egypt, struck a covenant with them and gave them the land of Canaan. He had punished them for their sins but would one day send them a Messiah. These and other convictions were endorsed by Christ and the early Church. The scriptures which recorded them were taken up into the biblical canon. But the precise way in which these convictions about God and his relation to men arose is far from clear. We might think predominantly of dramatic personal encounters with the self-disclosing God and of striking interventions in the course of political and social events. If this is our emphasis, almost inevitably we will contrast Israel's knowledge of and faith in God with those of her neighbours. Here would be something that transcended the environment and stood in opposition to the current religious culture. Our stress would be on the uniqueness of the religion – the doctrine, worship and ethic – which arose from the special divine self-communication to the Israelites. On the other hand we might care to reckon more with the possibility that Israel's convictions about the divine reality emerged progressively from a long mature reflection, in which there would be comparatively few moments of dramatic divine self-disclosure. Given this approach we would be more willing to think of revelation being mediated through the whole environment of the ancient near East. By interaction with her neighbours Israel could have grown in her knowledge of God.

Whichever way we prefer to understand the origins of Israel's faith in the self-revealing God, it is deeply concerned with prophets, and covenant, in particular the Sinai covenant. So far our remarks on covenant and prophets have been incidental to other themes. Let us now consider explicitly their relationship to revelation.

Yahweh's word and his saving acts stand in an intrinsic connection with the Sinai covenant; he reveals himself as the God of the covenant. In the tradition his speaking to Moses and the events of the exodus are closely linked with the covenant account and form the prologue to it. The divine intervention prepares the way for the covenant and forms the basis for the obedience required: 'I am the Lord your God, who brought you out of the land of Egypt, out of the land of bondage. You shall have no other gods before me' (Exod 20. 2f.).

The covenant itself comes from the free initiative of God; it is the gracious making known of his will, his gift to the people whom he has elected. Completely unequal 'partners' to this contract, they acknowledge the divine offer. It is in their acceptance of the saving revelation made by the covenant-God that they properly become the people of God.

> And Moses went up to God, and the Lord called to him out of the mountain, saying, 'Thus you shall say to the house of Jacob, and tell the people of Israel: You have seen what I did to the Egyptians, and how I bore you on eagles' wings and brought you to myself. Now therefore, if you will obey my voice and keep my covenant, you shall be my own possession among all peoples; for all the earth is mine, and you shall be to me a kingdom of priests and a holy nation. These are the words which you shall speak to the children of Israel' (Exod 19. 3-6).

It is by the covenant-revelation that the Israelites became God's holy nation. They accept their obligations to the covenant-making Lord, promising to remain loyal and to persist in living communion with him. Subsequent deeds and words of God look back to the covenant. He is proving his fidelity to the covenant, punishing the people who break the covenant and recalling them to their covenant obedience.

In their life as God's people the Israelites were affected by the functions of such classes as priests, judges, kings and prophets. We can consider here only the role of the prophets, i.e. the prophets who first appear with the period of the kings. We have already seen something of the revelation communicated through Moses, who was looked on both as the first prophet (Deut 18. 15, 18) and more exalted than the prophets (Num 12. 6ff.). What then is the prophetic function in Old Testament revelation? There is a twofold aspect to the prophet's role: he is a seer and a speaker. He perceives the truth of reality, above all what is really involved in the present life of the people, king and priests. He sees, e.g., the emptiness that lies behind the

23

façade of religiosity. Then too he is a divine spokesman (cf. 1 Sam 3. 19ff.), urging the people to be genuinely true to their covenant obligations, warning them against false security and showing the courage to denounce their sins. In need he intercedes for them; in disaster he comforts them. But in particular what is his role in mediating revelation? What does he contribute here?

The prophet interprets the meaning of the events which Israel experiences. These events may carry a God-given meaning, but they require the prophetic word for their explicit and authentic interpretation. Thus a prophet will understand a catastrophe not as a secular disaster, but as a divine punishment for sin, i.e. as an event of revelation. He sees God's on-going activity as connected with and as a continuation of the acts by which the Lord delivered Israel from Egypt. He will not merely unfold the meaning of such events as divine mercy and judgment, but will point to what is coming. There is to be a new saving covenant between God and man.

> 'Behold, the days are coming, says the Lord, when
> I will make a new covenant with the house of Israel
> and the house of Judah, not like the covenant which
> I made with their fathers when I took them by the
> hand to bring them out of the land of Egypt, my
> covenant which they broke, though I was their
> husband, says the Lord. But this is the covenant
> which I will make with the house of Israel after those
> days, says the Lord: I will put my law within them,
> and I will write it upon their hearts; and I will be their
> God, and they shall be my people' (Jer 31. 31-3).

The time of disaster and captivity becomes the occasion for the prophets to proclaim the time of salvation which is the goal of the divine plans. There is Ezekiel's vision of the valley of dry bones which the Spirit of the Lord will bring to life (37. 1-14). The people who have been driven into exile in Babylon will experience a new exodus (Is 40. 1ff.) and will be led into a new land (Is 43. 1ff.). Salvation is to come and it will be a universal salvation: 'My house shall be called a house of prayer for all peoples. Thus says the Lord God' (Is 56. 7f.; cf. Jer 16. 19).

In general it makes good sense to understand the prophetic role primarily in connection with promise. This view of revelation in terms of promise will be taken up later. The details of the prophets' message, however, involve us in many difficulties. To take one example. Isaiah proclaims a coming king like David but surpassing him in power, one who will enjoy 'the spirit of wisdom and understanding' (11. 1ff.; cf. 7, 11). Ezekiel announces that God himself will rescue the scattered sheep of his flock and 'set up over them one shepherd, my servant David' (34. 23). Second Isaiah speaks of the Lord's servant (42), the suffering man of sorrows (53). Daniel's vision concerns the Son of man coming down from heaven (7). To what extent did these various prophets envisage a single person to come? In what way may their different messages be interpreted as all concerned with the same person? (These classic and complicated issues will be considered in those later volumes in this series which deal with inspiration and the Old Testament.) Christians may understand Jesus of Nazareth as the son of David, the good shepherd, the suffering servant and Daniel's Son of man. But they should remember that they are looking back on a revelation which remained partial and fragmentary until the coming of the Son himself. 'In many and various ways God spoke of old to our fathers by the prophets; but in these last days he has spoken to us by a Son, whom he appointed the heir of all things, through whom also he created the world' (Heb 1. 1f.).

CHAPTER 2

CHRIST AND REVELATION

The deity of Christian revelation is known to us not just as the God of Abraham, Isaac and Jacob; he is the Father of Our Lord Jesus Christ. The last phrase reminds us that this revelation in history is not merely stretched out in space and time, but reaches a definitive peak in the 'last' revelation to which the earlier revelations were directed. The past times in which God spoke in 'many and various ways' stand in contrast with the period which follows, viz. 'these last days' in which God 'spoke to us by a Son' (Heb 1. 1f.). The divine revelation in history is Christo-centric. The many mediators of Old Testament revelation find their goal in the great revealer, the one figure on whom the interest of the New Testament is uniquely concentrated, the historical figure of Jesus of Nazareth.

With his appearance 'the time is fulfilled and the kingdom of God is at hand' (Mk 1. 15). Revelation is here and now in the person of Jesus of Nazareth. The divine self-disclosure is no longer mediated through events and words which – as it were – make a certain independent sense apart from the person of the revealer. Jesus is one with what he does; in his healing deeds the kingdom of God has come upon us (Lk 11. 20). He is the message which he proclaims in a way which is not true of other teachers: 'You are not to be called rabbi; for you have one teacher... Neither be called masters, for you have one master, the Christ' (Mt 23. 8, 10). Where the prophets had introduced their words with a 'Thus says the Lord', Jesus makes no such distinction between his words and his person: '*I say to you*, till heaven and earth pass away, not an iota, not a dot, will pass from the law until all is accomplished' (Mt 5. 18); '*I say to you*, rise, take up your pallet and go home' (Mk 2. 11); '*I send you out* as sheep in the midst of wolves' (Mt 10. 16). Jesus' call to be converted to God ('the kingdom of God is at hand; repent and believe in the gospel' (Mk 1. 15) is in fact a call to discipleship, to 'follow him on the way' (Mk 10. 52; cf. 1. 17; 8. 34-8 etc.).

The Fourth Gospel

Christ's role as the unique, perfect revealer emerges clearly from St John's Gospel. 'No one has ever seen God; the only Son, who is in the bosom of the Father, he has made him known' (1. 18). He 'comes from above' and 'bears witness to what he has seen and heard' (3. 31f.). This sonship which Jesus discloses is portrayed in the fourth Gospel as a unique communion with the Father in knowledge, love, life and 'work'. He knows the Father who has sent him and brings the true and definitive knowledge of God. 'We speak of what we know, and bear witness to what we have seen' (3. 11). 'He who sent me is true,' Jesus proclaims, 'and I declare to the world what I have heard from him' (8. 26). With the Father he has an abiding bond of love (8. 29; 15. 9) and a full communion of life. Jesus and the Father 'are one' (10. 30). 'Do you not believe that I am in the Father and the Father in me? The words that I say to you I do not speak on my own authority; but the Father who dwells in me does his works' (14. 10). Jesus does what he sees the Father doing (5. 19); he performs the same works as the Father (5. 21).

What Jesus says in his function as revealer is equated with what he does. 'When you have lifted up the Son of

27

man, then you will know that I am he, and that I *do* nothing on my own authority but *speak* thus as the Father taught me' (8. 28). Jesus' works no less than his words have a revelatory force; the Evangelist sets them before us on the same level. 'The *words* that I *say* to you I do not *speak* on my authority; but the Father who dwells in me *does* his *works*' (14. 10). Sometimes – as in this passage – the stress lies on the revelation of the Father. At other times the emphasis is on the revelation of Jesus himself: 'then you will know that I am he' (8. 28).

It is such 'I am' statements that are characteristic of Jesus' self-revelation in the fourth Gospel. 'I am,' Jesus declares, 'the good shepherd, the door, the light, the bread which has come down from heaven, the resurrection, the way, the truth and the life.' The high-point of this self-disclosure is the absolute 'I am' (8. 28). This statement without a predicate recalls the self-portrayal of God in Exodus 3. 14. Jesus is the epiphany, the revelation of God. No one other than Jesus – whether before or after him – could say, 'He who has seen me has seen the Father' (14. 9). In Jesus the glory of God, the divine presence, is seen upon earth (1. 14). He is the Word of God without qualification; the Word who was with God and was God has become flesh and dwelt among us (1. 1, 14).

St Matthew's Gospel

In understanding the revelation given through Christ the different New Testament writers have their own characteristic points of view. Thus Matthew interprets Jesus' work in terms of the fulfilment of promises. Jesus is revealer in that he fulfils the promises that came through the prophets (4. 12ff. etc.); he does this by his preaching, his actions and his presence. The key to Jesus' preaching is the gospel of God's rule and kingdom (4. 23). He frees the notion of God's kingdom from the earthly, political and national interpretations of his contemporaries and expresses its universal religious implications. The kingdom is God's gracious turning towards man, the establishment of God's power as eternal life and freedom from the power of evil, sin and death. The condition of entry into the kingdom is repentance – a readiness to turn from self-sufficiency to recognize God's dominion, to become like a little child and to receive the kingdom as a gift. 'To you it has been *given* to know the secrets of the kindgom of heaven' (13. 11). As this kingdom of God is present in the person of Jesus, to be granted to know the kingdom is in fact to discern the secret of Jesus' person, to read the signs of his saving works. Through him sickness, sin, death and the forces of devil are overcome. The conclusion is drawn: 'if it is by the Spirit of God that I cast out demons, then the kingdom of God has come upon you' (12. 28; cf. Lk 17. 20).

To know God's kingdom is to recognize Jesus for what he is and act accordingly. Here is something more than a prophet. With the prophets the mission and message were greater than the men themselves, but Jesus is identical with his mission. In him 'something greater than the temple' is revealed (Mt 12. 6). He is the place of the particular and gracious presence of God. The secret of Jesus and the secret which is revealed in him is the secret of personal, divine authority. In Jesus' coming the saving divine presence is disclosed, and at the same time a demand is made known. The call to repentance and to receive the kingdom of God becomes in fact a demand to confess Jesus: 'Everyone who acknowledges me before men, I also will acknowledge before my Father who is in heaven; but whoever denies me before men, I also will deny before my

Father who is in heaven' (10. 32f.). Men's attitude towards Jesus now will determine their status in God's coming judgment. Jesus is revealed as the principle for assessing human action and the norm of final judgment. 'The King' will say to 'those at his right hand', 'Truly, I say to you, as you did it to one of the least of these my brethren, you did it to me' (Mt 25. 34, 40). Jesus stands in the place of God and his authority is seen as that of God himself (cf. the Sermon on the Mount). In him the personal presence of God has become an event in human history, so that he is disclosed as 'Emmanuel', 'God with us' (1. 23).

In Matthew there is one famous passage where the understanding of revelation is distinctly Johannine in tone. 'All things have been delivered to me by my Father; and no one knows the Son except the Father, and no one knows the Father except the Son and any one to whom the Son chooses to reveal him' (11. 27). All knowledge of God which men enjoy – even that of the prophets – is no knowledge when compared with the knowledge Jesus claims as Son. Here is a unique sonship like that described at length in John's Gospel. It is this Son who exclusively brings the revelation of the Father and is the revealer of God in person: 'No one knows the Father except the Son and any one to whom the Son chooses to reveal him.' In the words of the fourth Gospel Jesus is 'the true light that enlightens every man' (1. 9); 'no one comes to the Father, but by me' (14. 6). For Matthew as for John the divine revelation in history is thoroughly Christo-centric.

Self-revelation

Before exploring further what the New Testament has to say about revelation it may be as well to consider the advisability of speaking of the divine *self*-revelation, an expression which we have often used already. In modern theology it is a commonplace to describe revelation as God's *self*-revelation. Theologians of different traditions may differ widely in their account of how this revelation takes place, but on the fact that the divine disclosure is a self-communication there is practically unanimous agreement. This view is found in the writings of such theologians as Bultmann, Barth, Tillich, René Latourelle, Emil Brunner, Henri de Lubac, Wolfhart Pannenberg and Jürgen Moltmann – to mention a few important names. Chapter one of the second Vatican Council's *Constitution on Divine Revelation* begins: 'In his goodness and wisdom God chose to reveal himself and to make known to us the hidden purpose of his will.'

What is not commonly realized is that this talk of God's *self*-revelation owes a great deal of its popularity to the influence of Hegel and the Hegelians, Marheineke and Biedermann. The fact that an expression has been encouraged by German idealism doesn't mean, of course, that it is automatically wrong. To describe the revelation proclaimed by the gospels as self-revelation makes excellent sense. The precise expression is, however, lacking in scripture itself. In the bible – at least as far as terminology is concerned – God reveals someone (e.g. Jesus) or something (e.g. his justice, salvation, glory and power) or to someone (e.g. to an apostle). Thus he has revealed his Son to Paul (Gal 1. 16); he has manifested his righteousness (Rom 3. 21). But God is never described precisely as revealing 'himself'. He is always the subject, never the object of his own revealing action. The first passage which speaks of God's self-revelation as such occurs in the letter of St Ignatius of Antioch to the Magnesians (8. 2).

It would be a narrow practice to confine ourselves

31

merely to expressions found explicitly in scripture. The bible does record a reality which we can legitimately describe as God's 'self-revelation'. This is a valuable term to describe what St John means when he writes: 'No one has ever seen God; the only Son, who is in the bosom of the Father, he has made him known' (1. 18). To talk of self-revelation is to indicate that it is not a thing but the personal divine reality which becomes known to us. The term suggests the initiative of God who emerges from his transcendence to meet man and hints at the love involved in God thus making himself personally accessible. We disclose things to anyone, but ourselves only to those with whom we have – or wish to have – a meaningful relation of trust and love. In this sense revelation is an expression of trust and love: 'I have called you friends, for all that I have heard from my Father I have made known to you' (15. 15). At the same time, however, 'self-revelation' – like all theological terms – is far from describing adequately the reality it is concerned with. In the encounter between the revealing God and the believing man more than divine self-revelation takes place; it is not merely God who is 'revealed' but also concomitantly man. Man is shown up for what he is; it takes this encounter with the divine revelation for man to be disclosed in his poverty, sin and misery before God. Through the revelation of the risen Christ Paul recognizes the evil of his former life and his utter dependence upon divine grace (1 Cor 15. 8-10; Gal 1. 13-16; Phil 3. 4ff.). Even as he is known by God he now knows himself in faith through God's eyes.

Closely allied with the talk of God's 'self-revelation' is the widespread twentieth-century understanding of revelation as an 'I-Thou encounter'. This expression – so much encouraged by the influence of Martin Buber and Ferd. Ebner – reminds us that revelation is not primarily a transaction between a personal subject and some 'material' object, some 'thing', but it is a subject to subject encounter. In making known his Father and himself Christ can say, '*I* have called *you* friends'. The 'I-Thou' account of revelation hints at its mysteriousness. In the communication of one human mind to another there is a hiddenness which defies, or at least can never be adequately conveyed by precise, rational analyses. All the more is this true of the encounter in which one of the 'subjects' is the invisible God made known to us by the 'Son who is in the bosom of the Father'.

In understanding the divine self-revelation on the model of a human 'I-Thou' encounter we must recall that in the act of revelation the triune God is already part of the human 'I'. In the fourth Gospel the incredulous see in Christ's works the extraordinary element (6. 2; 11. 47; 12. 18). But the mere seeing of Christ's miracles – even the raising of Lazarus from the dead – does not by itself lead to that believing encounter in which Christ's identity is acknowledged in faith (12. 37). Only those already 'drawn' by the Father recognize the presence and personal action of the Son of God (6. 44, 65). God must be at work on the human 'I' before it encounters in faith the divine 'Thou'. The first Gospel makes the same point when Jesus indicates the divine action that was the precondition of Peter's acknowledgment of him as Messiah: 'Blessed are you, Simon Bar-Jona! For flesh and blood has not revealed this to you, but my Father who is in heaven' (16. 17). This is a point to which we shall return later when treating of the acceptance of revelation. It is enough to note here the qualification that must be attached to an account of revelation as an 'I-Thou' encounter.

CHAPTER 3

CHRIST AND REVELATION (cont.)

We have been looking at the New Testament presentation of revelation, starting from the understanding of revelation we find in John and Matthew. A further step in our examination is to develop some of the characteristic themes to be found in various New Testament passages. In this chapter we discuss (a) revelation in creation, (b) revelation and Christ's death and resurrection and (c) the definitiveness of the revelation in Christ.

Revelation in Creation

The classic statement on revelation in creation comes in Romans 1. 18-23.

> For the wrath of God is revealed from heaven against all ungodliness and wickedness of men who by their wickedness suppress the truth. For what can be known about God is plain to them, because God has shown it to them. Ever since the creation of the world his invisible nature, namely, his eternal power and deity, has been clearly perceived in the things that have been made. So they are without excuse; for although they knew God they did not honour him as God or give thanks to him, but they became futile in their thinking and their senseless minds were darkened. Claiming to be wise, they became fools, and exchanged the glory of the immortal God for images resembling mortal man or birds or animals or reptiles.

In this passage Paul sees God as the invisible Lord who has come forth from his hiddenness. Since the creation of the world he has made himself known through his works. Nature is not eternally there, but is the work of God and has a beginning. God stands over against the created world; he is distinct from his works. In its character as created this world – and man along with it – discloses God. Man can know himself then as a creature and thus know his creator. There is a revelation of God's will in man himself, in the conscience which guides and obliges him (Rom 2. 14-16). From 'nature', i.e. on the basis of the human existence which God has created, the gentiles can 'do the works of the law'. This revelation of God in creation and within man himself is there to be recognized before our eyes, providing an abiding possibility of knowing God. 'The living God', Paul explains to the people of Lystra, 'who made the heaven and the earth and the sea and all that is in them ... did not leave himself without witness. For he did good and gave you from heaven rains and fruitful seasons, satisfying your hearts with food and gladness' (Acts 14. 15, 17). The rhythm of nature's seasons is the gift and the manifestation of God.

In fact men have failed *vis-à-vis* this revelation offered them in creation, and it is on the failure rather than the opportunity that Paul's emphasis lies in Romans 1. Although God is recognizable, men did not acknowledge, honour and thank him, but tried to live from themselves and their own achievements. They despised and falsified the truth about God's power and nature which was there to be acknowledged in the created world.

Two final remarks on Paul's statement on revelation in Romans 1. 18ff. There is no suggestion here – nor in Vatican I's use of the passage – that those who can or do come to know something of God from the works of creation reach this knowledge without the gracious divine help. Paul's concern is not with the presence or absence of such assistance but with the means of God's self-communication. He is discussing the case of those for whom revelation was mediated through the visible works of creation rather than through the events of Israel's history, the words of the prophets, the Christ-event and the apostolic proclamation. Secondly, for Paul the folly of those described in Romans 1. 18ff. does not consist in the fact that they tried to know God through creation. Their sin was that they despised and falsified the disclosed truth.

A more sympathetic view of man's failure to appreciate the revelation given in creation is found in the book of Wisdom. Like Paul the author asserts the possibility of recognizing God from the things he has made: 'From the greatness and beauty of created things comes a corresponding perception of their Creator' (13. 5). Man has in fact failed and is to be blamed, but he is not totally and exclusively blameworthy. 'Yet these men are little to be blamed, for perhaps they go astray while seeking God and desiring to find him. For as they live among his works they keep searching' (13. 6f.). The speech attributed to Paul in Acts 17 presents a similar positive view. He recognizes his hearers as God-fearing men and seizes on the fact that they have erected an altar 'to the unknown God'. What they have honoured without clear knowledge Paul now proclaims. In the errors of their religion he detects the trace of truth; he now calls on them to pass from that obscure intimation to clear recognition. In Romans he begins from an indictment of guilt and perversion. In Acts he uses the Athenians' genuine search for God as the setting for his proclamation of the true God, the Father of our Lord Jesus Christ.

We could look on the various religions of humanity as

reflecting and expressing the 'natural' revelation of God. They document what men in the course of history have in fact made of this divine disclosure either by way of receiving it faithfully or by turning it into error. Some of those who had a particularly intensive experience of this revelation became the founders of religions and religious communities. Nature religions with all their insights as well as their perversions reflect men's response to the revelation in the works of creation. Legal religions are a sign and witness of God's self-disclosure in the human conscience. The religions of redemption – with their myths of a lost paradise, man's guilt and divine punishment – express human longing for a saving revelation.

At the coming of Christ the divine revelation in creation is understood to be realized in a new way. It is the glory of the creator God which gleams on the face of Christ: 'It is the God who said, "Let light shine out of darkness," who has shone in our hearts to give the light of the knowledge of the glory of God in the face of Christ' (2 Cor 4. 6). Instead of describing Christ as definitively superseding the revelation given in the created works of God the New Testament sees him as the fulfilment of this revelation, the goal of creation: 'He is the image of the invisible God, the first-born of all creation' (Col 1. 15). The revelatory quality of creation reaches its climax in Christ. He is the highest perfection of creation, the true man, the second (and greater) Adam (cf. 1 Cor 15. 21f.; 45-49). Where the first Adam was made in the image and likeness of God (Gen 1. 26), Christ is incomparably more than that. He is the creator-God now present; he stands disclosed as the agent of (past) creation. 'He was in the beginning with God; things were made through him, and without him was not anything made that was made' (Jn 1. 1f.; cf. Heb 1. 2). Christ is revealed as both the cause as well as the goal of creation: 'all things were created through him and for him' (Col 1. 16).

Revelation, Death and Resurrection

In the divine self-revelation which Christ brings the supreme event is his death and resurrection. We can indicate this briefly from the fourth Gospel and the writings of St Paul. From the prologue of the fourth Gospel it could seem that the incarnation is the most relevant moment in St John's understanding of revelation. The pre-existent 'Word became flesh and dwelt among us, full of grace and truth; we have beheld his glory, glory as of the only Son from the Father' (1. 14). The prologue concludes: 'no one has ever seen God; the only Son, who is in the bosom of the Father, he has made him known' (1. 18). It looks as if we are being presented here with an incarnational view of the divine self-revelation in Christ. The Gospel, however, goes on to put the emphasis elsewhere. The 'signs' of Jesus' words and (miraculous) works fail to create general belief (12. 37ff.), so that it remains for his death and resurrection to mediate the revelation he brings.

St John seizes on the ambiguity of the word 'lift up' to indicate both the crucifixion and the exaltation of the risen Lord. 'Jesus said: "When you have lifted up the Son of Man, then you will know that I am he, and that I do nothing of my own authority but speak thus as the Father taught me"' (8. 28). It is this 'lifting up' which will disclose the secret of *Jesus*' person. It is by the 'coming' of the risen Lord to his disciples and their 'seeing' him that they will identify him; 'in that day you will know that I am in my Father' (14. 20). The death and resurrection reveal too the extent of Christ's loving obedience towards his Father.

After the Last Supper he declares: 'I do as the Father has commanded me, so that the world may know that I love the Father. Rise, let us go hence' (14. 31). Lastly it is in the context of his death and resurrection that we learn of Jesus' selfless love for men and his call to a responding love. The death and raising of Lazarus are not merely the climax of Jesus' ministry in the fourth Gospel but also the anticipation of what lay ahead for him. Here for the first time we read explicitly of Jesus' love for man; 'now Jesus loved Martha and her sister and Lazarus' (11. 5). At the sight of Jesus' tears over the death of Lazarus 'the Jews said, "See how he loved him!"' (11. 36). On Calvary Jesus gives his mother into the care of 'the disciple whom he loved' (19. 26). The death which follows is the greatest love that any man can show (15. 13). The risen Lord can call for love in return for the love which he has manifested: 'Simon, son of John, do you love me?' (21. 15ff.; cf. 14. 18-24).

In the fourth Gospel Jesus reveals God, his nature, his gracious gifts and his demands; this revelatory function reaches its climax in the crucifixion and resurrection. The same point is made by St Paul for whom the earthly ministry of Jesus obviously does not have the importance which it has, for example, in the first Gospel. In Paul's letters there is an almost total lack of material dealing with Jesus' ministry. Occasionally he echoes Jesus' moral teaching (cf. Rom 12. 14, 17; 13. 8-10). However we explain this phenomenon, it means that Jesus' ministry cannot be central to the Pauline understanding of revelation. What then does Paul have in mind when he writes of 'the light of the knowledge of God's glory in the face of Christ' (2 Cor 4. 4)? The epistle to the Galatians supplies the answer which can be readily confirmed elsewhere. God revealed his Son to Paul (1. 16) as that Son who 'gave himself for our sins' (1. 4; cf. 2. 20) by becoming 'a curse for us' and hanging upon the tree (3. 13) and being raised by the Father from the dead (1. 1). This good news about Christ's death and resurrection 'came through a revelation of Jesus Christ' (1. 12). This is the gospel which Paul sets before the Corinthians ('so we preach and so you believed' (1 Cor 15. 11)) and which is accepted in justifying faith: 'If you confess with your lips that Jesus is Lord and believe in your heart that God raised him from the dead, you will be saved' (Rom 10. 9). Earlier in Romans Paul describes the divine revelation as disclosing justification through faith: 'Now the righteousness of God has been manifested ... the righteousness of God through faith in Jesus Christ for all who believe' (3. 21f.). This faith is reckoned to us as righteousness if we 'believe in him that raised from the dead Jesus our Lord, who was put to death for our trespasses and raised for our justification' (4. 22-25). Christ's death and resurrection is clearly central to Paul's understanding of revelation as well as to his doctrine of faith. Later we will discuss the relation of revelation and faith and further aspects of Paul's understanding of revelation. It is enough to stress here that for St Paul even more than for St John the crucifixion and resurrection are essential to the recognition of God's revelation in Christ.

The Definitiveness of the Revelation

The divine self-revelation through Jesus of Nazareth is definitive, the 'last' revelation to which the earlier revelations were directed. '*Now* the righteousness of God has been manifested ... the righteousness of God through faith in Jesus Christ' (Rom 3. 21f.). This 'now' is the goal of God's previous self-communication and the future is nothing but the future of this 'now' in Christ.

There are many ways in which we can express to ourselves the definitiveness of this revelation. The divine Word has become flesh and dwelt among us (Jn 1. 1-14). 'In these last days God has spoken to us by a Son' (Heb 1. 2). God has no further word to say to us, no further one to send to dwell among us, for he has already 'given his only Son' (Jn 3. 16). Revelation could not go beyond this personal presence of the God-man, Jesus of Nazareth.

In Jesus is established and disclosed a 'new and eternal covenant' ratified between God and his people. Reflection on the function of Jesus as 'mediator' of this new covenant brings out the definitiveness of his work as revealer. Christ has been manifested as 'a high priest of the good things to come' (9. 11), who has mediated the covenant by shedding his blood (9. 15-22). 'He has appeared once for all at the end of the age to put away sin by the sacrifice of himself' (9. 26) and to purify our 'consciences from dead works to serve the living God' (9.14). It is on this definitiveness of Christ's role as founder of the 'new and eternal covenant' that Vatican II reflects: 'The Christian dispensation, therefore, as the new and definitive covenant, will never pass away, and we now await no further new public revelation before the glorious manifestation of our Lord Jesus Christ' (*Divine Revelation* 1. 4).

Finally we can understand in Matthean terms the definitive nature of the revelation in Christ. We have already noted how the first Gospel understands Jesus as revealer in that he fulfils the promises given through the prophets. His is a revelation of fulfilment which corresponds to a prior revelation of promise.

Along such lines we can reflect on revelation as finally given in Christ. Such reflection, however, does not exclude the end-revelation still to come. In fact where the New Testament speaks explicitly of revelation it does so predominantly in terms of this future revelation which is the second coming, the consummation of Christ's work. 'The *revealing of* our Lord Jesus Christ' will be on 'the day' of his final coming (1 Cor 1. 7f.), 'when the Lord Jesus is *revealed* from heaven' (2 Thess 1. 7). Now we await 'our blessed hope' which is 'the *appearing* or the glory of our great God and Saviour Jesus Christ' (Tit 2. 13). For 'Christ, having been offered once to bear the sins of many, will *appear a second time*, not to deal with sin but to save those who are eagerly waiting for him' (Heb 9. 28).

Between the present revelation given with Christ's death and resurrection and the revelation to come there is continuity. 'Now we see in a mirror dimly, but then face to face. Now I know in part; then I shall understand fully' (1 Cor 13. 12). The revelation we experience will be consummated by the revelation we await. St Paul expresses his hope for a divine disclosure which he expects as the saving act of God at the end of time. In waiting for the redemption in which 'the revealing of the sons of God' (Rom 8. 19) will occur he is conscious too that he has already an anticipated, provisional possession of this final saving revelation. We enjoy 'the first fruits of the spirit' (Rom 8. 23) in being and knowing that we are 'children of God', even if we must still await 'the glory that is to be revealed to us' (Rom 8. 16, 18).

The final revelation is that consummation of God's rule for which we pray, 'Thy kingdom come' (Mt 7. 10) and 'Come, Lord Jesus' (Apoc 22. 20; 1 Cor 16. 22). This revelation will be the unambiguous manifestation of God's glory to the world in the final judgment and the resurrection of the dead. Then Christ will deliver the kingdom to his Father, when all evil is manifestly overcome and all things are subjected to the Son (1 Cor 15. 20-28).

CHAPTER 4

CHRIST, THE HOLY SPIRIT AND THE APOSTLES

Clearly our understanding of the divine self-manifestation in Christ involves us in a discussion of the sending of the Holy Spirit. We have noted how in the fourth Gospel the climax of Christ's role as revealer is reached when he is 'lifted up' in his crucifixion and resurrection. That is precisely the moment when from Christ's side there comes forth the water, the symbol of the Spirit (19. 34; 7. 37-9). It is the Holy Spirit which is the gift of the risen Lord to his apostles (20. 22). What then is the connection between the revelation in Christ and the coming of the Spirit?

The Holy Spirit is to preserve and continually make accessible the saving revelation given with Christ: 'He will bring to your remembrance', Christ guarantees, 'all that I have said to you' (Jn 14. 26). Through the Spirit the truth of Jesus' identity continues to be known: 'No one can say "Jesus is Lord" except by the Holy Spirit' (1 Cor 12. 3). It is the Spirit who determines the inner nature of Christian existence in which by faith, hope, love and prayer we recognize God our Father made known to us through his Son. Paul affirms that God has revealed his Son to him and that it is this revealed gospel which he preaches to others (Gal 1. 11-16). This saving revelation comes about, he explains, in that 'God has sent the Spirit of his Son into our hearts, crying "Abba! Father!"' (Gal 4. 6; cf. Rom 8. 15f.). It is this same Spirit who builds into a unity those who believe in the manifestation of Jesus as the Lord (1 Cor 12. 3ff.).

We must further clarify the connection between the

revelation in Christ and the Holy Spirit. But first we should take into account the role of the apostles in revelation.

The apostles and their ministry – above all their proclamation – belong uniquely to the event or revelation in Christ. In an unrepeatable way they stand with Christ the divine revealer; his work is not done without them. 'Go therefore and make disciples of all nations ... teaching them to observe all that I have commanded you' (Mt 28. 19f.). The apostles, the official witnesses of Christ's resurrection, provide the bridge from him to humanity. To them God is revealed in his Son; their mission is that of being proclaiming witnesses to this revelation. Peter stands up 'with the eleven' (Acts 2. 14) to preach the revealing event which is Christ's death, and resurrection, made known with the sending of the Holy Spirit. It is this proclamation which shapes the Church, building the community of those who believe in Jesus as the Lord. To all the apostles we can apply the words of 1 Jn 1. 2-3: 'the life was made manifest, and we saw it, and testify to it, and proclaim to you the eternal life which was with the Father and was made manifest to us – that which we have seen and heard we proclaim also to you, so that you may have fellowship with us; and our fellowship is with the Father and with his Son Jesus Christ.' In its various written forms the apostolic witness – whether written directly by the apostles themselves or by someone in apostolic circles – makes up the canon of New Testament scriptures. Their preaching and the articulation of their faith which in different ways are recorded in the books of New Testament are acknowledged in the Church as the normative account of the revelation in Christ. This revelation which was mediated through the apostles, called forth faith and gave rise to the Christian Church we can call foundational revelation.

One important question arises at this point in our discussion: when did the (foundational) revelation to the apostles come to an end? Did it continue through the lives of the apostles until the end of the so-called apostolic age? After Pentecost were they the recipients of further 'revelations' – not from the earthly or the risen Jesus, but from the Holy Spirit? It seems to fit the data of the New Testament better to hold that the unique foundational revelation to the apostles closed with the end of Christ's visible presence. The appearances of the risen Lord to the official apostolic witnesses (Acts 1. 21f.; 1 Cor 15. 8) set the limits; there were no further revelations which – as it were – completed the 'content' of the revelation in Christ. To his apostles Jesus had made known everything (Jn 15. 15). In him the truth of God was present in its fullness so that Christ could simply say, 'I am the truth' (Jn 14. 6). He is the unique mediator of revelation as he is of salvation. How could we reconcile that with a view of immediate revelations by the Holy Spirit to the apostles? In the first Gospel the closing command of Christ is to proclaim what he has taught (28. 19); the risen Lord makes the word of the historical Jesus normative for the apostles and the Church on earth till the end of time.

At the same time, however, it is obvious that the apostles come in the course of decades to an understanding of revelation which was not possible during the time of Christ's visible presence. Through their reflection they reach a clearer articulation of the revelation which had been given to them. The function of the Holy Spirit is to help them in this evolving interpretation and growth in understanding. The Spirit is to recall what Christ has communicated and lead to the truth which the apostles received without properly grasping it (Jn 14. 26; 16. 13).

It is important to distinguish the apostles' reflections from those of later Christian thinkers. God guarantees the truth of the apostolic articulation of the revelation recorded in the New Testament scriptures. The Church has always been convinced that the apostles enjoy a unique role as true witnesses. Their special function as 'founding fathers' carries with it a special guarantee. Their trustworthiness affects not merely their proclamation of the revealing event in Christ but also their further interpretation on the basis of meditation and reflection under the Holy Spirit.

In our understanding of the apostles' role we should not assume that their continuing exercise of authority which can be definitively binding on the Church requires a continuance of revelation. They may take decisions which the Church acknowledges as irreversible, e.g. regarding the imposition of hands for the communication of the Holy Spirit. But there is no need to postulate a special revelation behind that decision. Furthermore, we need to distinguish the closing of foundational revelation from the coming into being of the Church. Such revelation ends – we have argued – with the withdrawal of Christ's visible presence. The Church is in a sense already there as soon as the Lord appears to Peter and he gathers about him the other apostles (Lk 24. 34; 1 Cor 15. 5). Yet the Church is not fully constituted until the end of the apostolic period. The process of fully establishing the Church and the taking of irrevisible apostolic decisions go on then beyond the time when foundational revelation ends, viz. when the risen Lord withdraws his visible presence from his apostles.

CHAPTER 5

FAITH, ST PAUL AND SALVATION

So far we have often mentioned man's faith as the response which the divine revelation calls forth. Thus many of the Samaritans, confronted by the revealing word, come to belief (Jn 4. 39-42). Faith as the correlate of God's self-disclosure is the first topic for consideration in this chapter.

Faith

Although it is not man's achievement but God's act, revelation is not given until recognized and accepted by man. God's self-manifestation does not, as it were, hang in the void. It is not simply 'there', like some static, independent thing which could be thought of and become the object of human attention as if it were something 'out there' or 'back there'. A revelation in which someone or something is not revealed for somebody would simply be no revelation. There is no such thing as revelation by itself. Christ the revealer, God the revealed and man as the one to whom the revelation is given belong together in an inseparable unity. St Paul writes of God revealing his Son (Gal 1. 16) and then speaks – equivalently – of the coming of faith (3. 23ff.). The divine revelation and the emergence of faith are the two sides of the same event. Revelation appears only in the event of faith, even though it is not reducible to this event.

To the divine self-communication corresponds man's self-commitment, his acceptance of a personal relationship with God. We cannot properly know or speak of revelation from a neutral, an uncommitted point of view. Revelation demands an intensely active participation, viz. the religious response of believing in the God who reveals himself. For it is a call to 'hearing' in that fuller sense which implies the obedience of faith. This is the sense of the Nicene and other traditional creeds. They are not primarily collections of dogmas but a means of expressing our common allegiance, trust and faith in the triune God of revelation. Our faith is directed towards God who has revealed his will to save us in Christ; it is not firstly knowledge, but acknowledgment. We firstly 'believe in'; only secondarily do we 'believe that'. In essence faith is not primarily holding correct doctrines or assenting to a collection of dogmatic propositions, but it consists in an obedient commitment to the self-revealing God. It is a personal response to the disclosed intentions of a personal being.

The faith that springs from encounter with revelation will articulate itself in statements of faith. Correct doctrine will genuinely, if always inadequately, represent and assist this living commitment. Incorrect doctrine will misrepresent, hinder or prevent it.

If faith as obedient commitment is the correlate of revelation, revelation is 'now' even as faith is 'now'. Revelation will be a living, present reality, a contemporary event which takes place. It will be found only in the living man, the recipient without whom it will not exist. Revelation is primarily 'now', not 'then' or 'back there' to a circle of privileged persons.

If this is so, what does it mean to talk about revelation 'closing' with the period of the apostles – whether we locate this 'closing' at the end of the apostolic age or earlier at the withdrawal from the apostles of the visible presence of the risen Lord? An answer to this question involves a distinction between what we could call 'foundational' and 'dependent' revelation. The revelation proclaimed by the apostles, the official witnesses of the risen Christ, gave rise to Christian faith and founded the Christian Church. Their lives and preaching are now over, but their witness remains as the normative account of the revelation in Christ. Dependent revelation began as soon as St Peter stood up with the eleven and proclaimed the crucified and risen Lord. It was dependent revelation which came to his hearers and which has been communicated since as an ever present, living renewal of the revelation enjoyed by the apostles. It is an encounter found 'now' with reference to the revelation that took place 'then'. Hence to talk about revelation 'closing' with the apostles is to give the historical reference of present, living revelation. In this sense revelation, like faith, is primarily now. But this present revelation remains always dependent; it looks back to the unique role of the apostles then.

In the fourth Gospel Jesus makes it clear not merely that the continuing experience of revelation is connected with the activity of the Holy Spirit. This present revealing also has always its reference to Jesus himself: 'The Holy Spirit, whom the Father will send in my name, he will teach you all things, and bring to your remembrance all that I have said to you' (14. 26). The experience now of God's self-communication through the Spirit is equivalent to that of being then with Jesus.

St Paul

The remarks above on revelation as a living, present reality link up with some aspects of the understanding of revelation to be found in St Paul. From among those letters which are generally agreed to come immediately from Paul himself four in particular (Romans, 1 and 2 Corinthians and Galatians) have particularly important things to say about the nature of revelation. We have already noted how the apostle writes sometimes about revelation as an event still to come, viz. with the last day (e.g. Rom 2. 5; 8. 19; 1 Cor 1. 7). His Damascus-road experience which he described sometimes as a vision (1 Cor 9. 1; 15. 8; cf. Acts 9. 3-9; 22. 6-11; 26. 12-18) he also styles a revelation: 'he who had set me apart before I was born, and had called me through his grace was pleased to reveal his Son to me' (Gal 1. 15 f.; cf. 1. 12). It is clear from Galatians that Jesus Christ is revealed as the Son of God who makes possible for man a divine sonship: 'When the time had fully come, God sent forth his Son, born of woman, born under the law, to redeem those who were under the law, so that we might receive adoption as sons' (4. 5f.). Christ is manifested as the one who brings the time of justification which comes by faith and not through human achievements. In content Gal 1. 16 is the equivalent of Paul's later statement about the coming or the revelation of faith: 'before faith came, we were confined under the law, kept under restraint until faith should be revealed' (3. 23; cf. Rom 1. 17; 3. 21). Paul is the object of that gracious saving action of God which he can describe as a revelation of the Son (1. 16), the coming of faith (3. 23) and the sending of the Son to make our sonship possible (4. 5f.). Revelation is then for Paul something more than Christ's death and resurrection as such. It is the action of God with reference to this death and resurrection in conveying to man the significance of the Christ-event as it affects man for faith and salvation.

In speaking of the revelation he has received Paul's prime concern in Galatians is to validate the truth of his gospel and his own status as an apostle. How does he understand revelation when he is writing about others, the rank and file of the first Christian communities? On one point Paul is insistent. The revelation which Christians enjoy is not based on or equivalent to ecstatic visions and experiences. The opponents whom he criticizes in 2 Corinthians seem to have understood revelation as the knowledge of the identity of themselves as redeemed with the redeemer, *a knowledge which was demonstrated by means of ecstatic experiences.* These opponents force Paul to go more deeply into the question of revelation than he does in other letters. As a counter argument he reluctantly lays claim, it is true, to a high degree of ecstatic experience (12. 1ff.). But the event which he describes here is not his Damascus-road encounter. Nor is it modesty which makes Paul speak here in the third person ('I know a man in Christ who fourteen years ago was caught up to the third heaven'), but a conviction that such ecstasies are not the basis of his proclamation. Neither for him nor for others is revelation to be understood in terms of ecstasy. Paul views these ecstatic experiences as he does speaking in tongues (1 Cor 14. 2). They may have a meaning for the individual Christian's relation to God, but not for the community. In particular the role of an apostle as a witness of revelation is not to be judged by such experiences; Paul does not base his apostolic function on them. When 'beside himself' in his ecstasies he is united with God; when 'in his right mind' in his preaching he is united with the community (2 Cor 5. 13).

On the positive side how does Paul interpret the revelation which the Corinthians receive? It is something that becomes an event in their lives through the proclamation and life of the apostle. A passage like 2 Cor 2. 12-17 is illuminating in this regard. Through Paul God is 'revealing the odour of his knowledge' (v. 14) firstly by way of the apostle's proclamation. Paul preaches the word of God in all its purity and – unlike his opponents – does not act as a hawker, adulterating the message and concentrating his attention on financial gain (v. 17). The divine revelation takes place then through the apostolic preaching – a revelation which means salvation and life for those who accept it but ruin for those who refuse it (vv. 15, 16). The word of proclamation makes Jesus and his salvation present; it actually communicates the proclaimed reality to the believer. Paul's preaching is 'the message of reconciliation' through which men's sins are no longer counted against them and they become 'the righteousness of God' (2 Cor 5. 18-21). As his apostolic message of reconciliation has no meaning apart from the reconciling activity of God, the apostolic proclamation may be understood as 'working together with' God (2 Cor 6. 1). At Paul's proclamation of Jesus Christ crucified and risen (1 Cor 2. 2; 15. 1ff.) men find themselves through the power of God (1 Cor 1. 5) able to see and believe in Jesus as Lord (1 Cor 12. 3).

Another passage which is relevant at this point is Romans 10. 20: 'Then Isaiah is so bold as to say, "I have been found by those who did not seek me; I have shown myself to those who did not ask for me"'. Citing the text of Isaiah which was originally concerned with Israel Paul applies it to the revelation which has come to the gentiles. The context (10. 14ff.) shows clearly that this revelation occurs in and through the word of proclamation. This proclamation is no simple, disinterested account of past events. The word does not merely narrate, but creates a situation, carrying the present action of divine disclosure and address to the hearers.

In bringing to men the living reality which is revelation the (suffering) life of the apostle too has its function: 'We are afflicted in every way, but not crushed ... always carrying in the body the death of Jesus, so that the life of Jesus may also be manifested in our bodies' (2 Cor 4. 8, 10). All the various sufferings and tribulations of Paul's existence are the means of the divine revelation (cf. 2 Cor 6. 4-10; 11. 23-27; 1 Cor 4. 11-13). It is in these sufferings that the crucified Jesus is manifested as Lord.

To sum up Paul's doctrine. For him revelation is a saving action of God on the community here and now which takes place through both word and event,viz. the preaching and (suffering) existence of the apostle. Paul does recognize his Damascus-road experience as revelation, viz. as that revelation of the crucified and risen Lord which constitutes the foundational revelation to the apostles. But rather than think of revelation exclusively or even predominantly as some past event 'back there' which legitimizes the apostolic proclamation and ministry, Paul emphasizes the revelation here and now. It is a saving divine action on those to whom through word and event the death and resurrection of Christ become known. We have seen too how Paul also awaits a revelation as the saving act of God at the end of time. The revelation we now experience will be consummated by that revelation which we hope for. The characteristic Pauline interests are with revelation as (1) a present living reality which we experience and (2) a future grace that is longed for.

Revelation and Salvation

In the discussion of St Paul it should have been obvious that for him revelation and salvation mean in fact the same thing. God is revealing 'the fragrance' of his knowledge 'among those who are being saved' (2 Cor 2. 14f.).

The word of God's appeal comes through Paul to the Corinthians as the offer of salvation: 'Behold, now is the acceptable time; behold, now is the day of salvation' (2 Cor 6. 2). Conversely those who do not 'see the light of the gospel of the glory of Christ' are 'those who are perishing' (2 Cor 4. 3f.). God reveals himself in grace and judgment; hence failure to acknowledge the revelation offered is failure to find salvation. If 'the word of the cross' is 'the power of God to us who are being saved', it is 'folly to those who are perishing' (1 Cor 1. 18).

In considering the Epistle to the Galatians we have already seen how easily Paul slips from the revelation of the Son of God (1. 16) to the coming of saving faith (3. 23ff.) and the sending of the Son to effect our sonship (4. 4ff.). In such a passage as Romans 3. 21f. Paul draws together in a classic synthesis the notions of the righteousness of God which has been revealed and faith, man's response to this saving revelation: 'Now the righteousness of God has been manifested apart from the law... the righteousness of God through faith in Jesus Christ for all who believe'.

If we turn to modern times we can see how thoroughly salvific is the understanding of revelation in Vatican II. Take the opening sentence of chapter one of the *Constitution on Divine Revelation*:

> God chose to reveal himself and to make known to
> us the hidden purpose of his will by which through
> Christ, the Word made flesh, man has access to the
> Father in the Holy Spirit and comes to share in the
> divine nature.

There is no need to labour the point. If we read the rest of this opening chapter we can see in how many different ways it is indicated that revelation is salvific.

Revelation and salvation belong together; for the very fact that God speaks to man is itself a transforming grace.

God's word is living and effective (Is 55. 11; Heb 4. 12; 3. 7f.) and is never the mere passing on of information. From the beginning God's word is described in the scriptures as power-laden: 'God said, "Let there be light"; and there was light' (Gen 1. 3). Through Paul God's revealing word comes to his hearers: 'we are ambassadors for Christ, God making his appeal through us' (2 Cor 5. 20). The word is an effective call which creates a saving knowledge. If in faith we accept this 'enlightening' word we will find salvation (cf. Rom 10. 9; 2 Cor 4. 6).

In St John's Gospel the 'lifting up' of the crucifixion and resurrection is both revealing and saving. Jesus declares: 'When you have lifted up the Son of man, then you will know that I am he' (8. 28). He also promises, 'I, when I am lifted up, from the earth, will draw all men to myself' (12. 32). This 'lifting up' will bring through faith the life of grace (cf. 3. 14f.).

As with revelation there is the same tension between the salvation already given in Christ and that which has not yet come, between the 'now' and the 'then': 'Now we see in a mirror dimly, but then face to face' (1 Cor 13. 12). Even if Christ has truly communicated to us a saving knowledge of God, our experience of both salvation and revelation is characterized as anticipatory. 'Beloved, we are God's children now; it does not yet appear what we shall be, but we know that when he appears we shall be like him, for we shall see him as he is' (1 Jn 3. 2). The goal of our existence is to have that communion with God involved in seeing God as he is. We have already noted how such a passage as Romans 8. 15ff. draws together the notions of revelation and salvation in expressing a hope for that divine disclosure which will be the final saving act of God. The saving revelation we now enjoy will then be consummated.

Perhaps nowhere else in the New Testament can we

sense so keenly the tension between what has taken place and what will take place as in the Epistle to the Hebrews. On the one hand there is the stress on what has occurred: 'In these last days God has spoken to us by a Son' (1. 2). This Son has redeemed mankind by sharing in human nature 'that through death he might destroy him who has the power of death, that is, the devil, and deliver all those who through fear of death were subject to lifelong bondage (2. 14f.). On the other hand salvation is placed in the future at the final revelation which is the Son's second coming: 'Christ, having been offered once to bear the sins of many, will appear a second time, not to deal with sin but to save those who are eagerly waiting for him' (9. 28). Yet the 'now' and the 'then' do not merely stand in continuity but are in a sense one. The link is closer than, e.g., the link between the revelation given to Abraham and the revelation given through Christ; that was a relationship of promise and fulfilment. Here we have the fulfillment in Christ reaching its consumation. Here the progression is no movement from Abraham to Christ, but from Christ to Christ, from Christ risen to Christ finally manifested as having subjected all his enemies. The last day will bring no saving event to surpass that already mediated by Christ. For 'now the righteousness of God has been manifested... through faith in Jesus Christ' (Rom 3. 21f.). The future offers us nothing more than the future of this 'now' in Christ.

CHAPTER 6

OBSCURITY, ACCEPTANCE AND PROOF

The revelation to come will be the final divine saving action. This holds good whether we think of the individual at his death or human society at the end-time. The revelation to come will do away with what is characteristic of God's present self-manifestation, viz. that it is symbolic, obscure and ambiguous. In this chapter we discuss some further aspects of revelation, starting from this obscurity.

The Obscurity of Revelation

The revelation to come will be a person-to-person encounter in the fullest possible sense. It will be a continuing, direct, face-to-face knowing in which God will stand revealed with full clarity and intimacy. By way of contrast the present revelation falls well short of anything like complete disclosure. Like the salvation which we now enjoy the divine self-revelation is given only in a qualified sense. It is not there in fullness or certainty, but must be characterized as partial and obscure. 'Now we see in a mirror dimly... now I know in part' (1 Cor 13. 12). This means that the revelation of God in Christ can be overlooked, misunderstood and become the occasion for scandal and contradiction. 'The word of the cross' which Paul proclaims proves to some a stumbling-block and sheer folly (1 Cor 1. 18-25). It is not merely that the message preached is accessible only through the testimony of witnesses: 'God raised' Jesus of Nazareth 'on the third day', declares St Peter, 'and made him manifest; not to all the people but to us who were chosen by God as witnesses' (Acts 10. 40f.). The very gospel itself that is proclaimed can appear strange and deserving of mockery (Acts 17. 32). Paul admits that the 'wisdom' which he offers is not 'of this age'; 'we impart a secret and hidden wisdom of God'. To describe his gospel he makes use of the words of Isaiah: '"What no eye has seen, nor ear heard, nor the heart of man conceived, what God has prepared for those who love him," God has revealed to us' (1 Cor 2. 6f., 9f.). The strange paradox of God's revelation is that it was precisely when Jesus was 'made sin' and hung 'cursed upon the tree' that 'God was in Christ reconciling the world to himself' (Gal 3. 13; 2 Cor 5. 18-21). The dying of Jesus is the place where God's power is revealed. This means too that the very 'weakness' of Christ's apostles (2 Cor 10. 10) serves only to manifest God's action. The afflictions of the apostolic existence disclose the saving divine power (2 Cor 4. 7ff.). This then is the 'content' of the gospel which runs counter to human ways of thinking and explains why men may remain unmoved by the proclamation (1 Cor 1. 21). It is something obscure, even repellent; only in faith can the opposition to this message be overcome (1 Cor 2. 8).

When considering the paradoxical nature of the revelation through Christ, we should remember that this is not the same as the hiddenness, e.g., of the esoteric knowledge claimed by the Qumran sectarians. Here is no secret into which one can be initiated and which one can then fully grasp. Those who come to faith at the preaching of the gospel 'know' God in his self-revealing presence but only in the same darkness and hiddenness which characterizes our present participation in Christ's saving grace. 'You have died, and your life is hid with Christ in God. When Christ who is our life appears, then you also will appear with him in glory' (Col 3. 3f.).

The limited nature of the divine revelation means that God is not known in the overwhelming majesty of his glory and his will is not felt at full force. With the divine reality not presented openly and irresistibly, man is not compelled to accept God and to carry out his commands. Room is left for genuine obedience as well as for wilful refusal and failure to understand. Obedient faith as a response to divine revelation lives always by overcoming the abiding challenge left by the 'weakness' of God in his revelation. Our knowledge of the divine self-disclosure is great enough to enable us to serve God with loving, obedient faith. It is limited enough to leave us free to refuse.

To recognize revelation man must be ready to turn from his godlessness and sinfulness. He is not told 'See the truth' or 'Read history correctly,' but 'Repent'. The reality of revelation will remain a puzzle to sinful man so long as he refuses the grace of conversion.

The Acceptance of Revelation

What has just been said could suggest that man's failure to acknowledge God's self-revelation is simply an act of wilful human refusal. But this is in fact only one of the New Testament explanations for the non-recognition of revelation. It is the reason which seems foremost in the 'woes' that Christ pronounces over the cities 'where most of his mighty works had been done' (Mt 11. 20-24). It is the explanation underlying Paul's denunciation of those who have not acknowledged the Creator manifested 'in the things that have been made'; they 'are without excuse' (Rom 1. 20).

At the same time, however, the failure to hear the divine call and recognize the God who reveals himself in Christ is put down to the effect of satanic forces. In 2 Corinthians Paul ponders on the partial ineffectiveness of his preaching and wrestles with the problem of unbelief. He has preached the unvarnished truth of the gospel. Why don't all believe and see the revelation in Christ? One answer is that Satan, 'the god of this world, has blinded the minds of the unbelievers, to keep them from seeing the light of the gospel of the glory of Christ'. For them the gospel remains 'veiled' (4. 3f.; cf. Eph 2. 2). Considered in itself, revelation is a light which should shine into the heart. When the heart is not reached, it is no fault of the light; evil has blinded those for whom the light is intended. A similar view is expressed through the early Church's allegorizing of Jesus' parable of the sower. The evil one is likely to prevent those who hear the proclamation of the kingdom from recognizing God's word to them: 'When any one hears the word of the kingdom and does not understand it, the evil one comes and snatches away what is sown in his heart' (Mt 13. 19). Evil influences outside a man can prevent his believing acceptance of divine revelation.

There is a third explanation which the New Testament offers of man's faith or unfaith, viz. that God's initiative is paramount. Only those 'drawn' by the Father (Jn 6. 44, 65) can 'come' in faith to Christ. When Paul preaches the Christ-event, 'the word of God is at work' in those who come to believe (1 Thess 2. 13). When through Paul's proclamation men reach 'the knowledge of the glory of God in the face of Christ', this is due to God who once said, 'Let light shine out of darkness' and is now illuminating men's hearts to give them this knowledge by – as it were – a new act of creation (2 Cor 4. 6). Man's acceptance of revelation in faith is a work of God to be compared with the original creation. Knowing Christ in a life-giving way means that we are united to Christ as 'a new creation'. Our old life is over; a new life has begun. From first to last this is the work of God (2 Cor 5. 16-18). Our faith rests then on the power of God; it is God who 'has revealed to us through the Spirit' (1 Cor 2. 5, 10). In many different ways the New Testament forces upon us the role of the divine initiative in man's acceptance of God's self-communicating grace. The 'woes' pronounced in the first Gospel over the sinful cities would seem to highlight man's responsibility as the key factor, but almost immediately we read: 'No one knows the Father except the Son and any one to whom the Son chooses to reveal him' (11. 27). The classic discussion of this matter is given by St Paul in chapters 9-11 of Romans. No other section of the scriptures stresses more the sovereign free election of God who 'has mercy upon whomever he wills, and he hardens the heart of whomever he wills' (9. 18). Paul can only conclude with a cry of wonder before the mystery of God's electing call: 'How unsearchable are his judgments and how inscrutable his ways' (11. 33).

By way of accounting for human action in the face of divine revelation the New Testament speaks then of (1) man's free responsibility, (2) the influence of satanic forces of evil and (3) the supreme divine will. The three explanations simply lie side by side in the scriptures; no synthesis is given. But clearly the third is offered as the ultimate account; final explanations can lie only in God.

Proving Revelation

A question which obviously arises from the matter discussed in this chapter is: can we prove revelation? Are we able to demonstrate that in Jesus of Nazareth God has revealed himself? Is the divine self-disclosure the object of ordinary verification?

Many apologists both Catholic and non-Catholic have felt that to doubt or deny the demonstrable validity of the Christian gospel is to turn faith into a blind venture and a form of superstitious gullibility which involves intellectual suicide. They are confident that the methods of reason and historical science can verify the truth of revelation. Their proofs seem to them clear and convincing; on this case faith can be founded. Protected by this preliminary rational investigation Christian belief is shown not be arbitrary. It would seem to be only ignorance or prejudice which stops unbelievers from appreciating the force of their arguments.

Admittedly we have given here an over-simplified account of the position taken by these apologists. But something like that is the impression gained from many Catholic writers at least up to Vatican II, some Anglicans and from such a Lutheran author as Wolfhart Pannenberg. Their attempts, however, to prove revelation are unacceptable. If we insist on establishing revelation through normal methods of verification, we turn our knowledge of the God who reveals himself in Christ into something achieved by our own efforts. Our grasp of the divine self-disclosure would become our own work instead of being acknowledged as a gift that comes through gracious divine intervention. We would ground faith on human intellectual achievement. Paul, however, insists with the Corinthians that their faith does 'not rest in the wisdom of men but in the power of God' (1 Cor 2. 5).

One could object that there are many people who have come to Christian faith after a long period of study, discussion, examination of history, etc. Even in such cases, however, it would be illusory to think that faith was something reached through the process of normal verification and built on naturally gained human knowledge. Right from the very outset of such persons' investigations and first steps towards faith God's grace is at work. Without divine assistance man cannot take a single step towards the believing acknowledgment of God's saving revelation in Christ. Even striking miraculous signs by themselves will not bring an insight into God's presence in Christ. Revelation cannot be proved or forced on man in that fashion by the miraculous.

On the other hand we should not deny that the situation of faith responding to revelation is at least a partially intelligible reality. It is not a blind leap in the dark. After all the apostles had some describable, understandable message to proclaim. There was something to be 'known'. (We should recognize, of course, that in the scriptures 'knowing' has a wider sense than merely grasping intellectually; it includes such notions as loving recognition, obeying etc... Even so biblical knowing does retain a rational, intelligible dimension.) St Paul could pass readily from talking of faith and believing to speak of seeing or knowing. '*Unbelievers*' are those who are kept from '*seeing* the light of the gospel of the glory of Christ' and do not come to 'the *knowledge* of the glory of God in the face of Christ' (2 Cor 4. 4, 6; cf. 4. 13f.). As 1 Cor 1. 21 implies, to believe is to know the divine revelation: 'For since, in the wisdom of God, the world did not *know* God through wisdom, it pleased God through the folly of what we preach to save those who *believe*.' The man who comes to know the divine self-revelation can then express his experience in intelligible statements. As a believer he does not remain dumbly imprisoned in his own inarticulate subjectivity. He can talk about what revelation means for him, stating simply what has happened to him in the Christian community, how he came to believe and how he reasons about things from the position of faith. Thus he can give some kind of rational account of the living, personal reality which is divine revelation. But this is not to say that he can adopt a neutral, uncommitted point of view and show that revelation can be proved. We are dealing here with an event of 'seeing' and 'knowing' that occurs through the loving kindness of God and is not something which can be effected by mere rational investigation and demonstration. At the same time, of course, this 'seeing' and 'knowing' does not remain a private assurance which is not subject to criticism. It is checked, directed and corrected not merely by the written record of revelation in the scriptures, but also by the living experience of others in the Christian community who enjoy a similar experience of the divine revelation.

CHAPTER 7

THE CHURCH

In an earlier chapter we considered how with the coming of Christ revelation reached a definitive goal. '*Now* the righteousness of God has been manifested ... through faith in Jesus Christ' (Rom 3. 21f.). The future will bring nothing more than the future of this 'now' in Christ, the ever-continuing actualization of this divine disclosure, the constant living renewal of the revelation to the apostles. In this on-going re-enactment of the revelatory event what is the function of the Church? How do we understand the enduring Church *vis-à-vis* the continuing reality of reve-lation?

The Church is a world church with a salvific ministry for all humanity, viz. to set before all men God's will to save in Christ. It is the 'place' of revelation. Through the witness of the Church men encounter Christ as the revelation of God's merciful love. In subordination to the foundational apostolic witness the Church makes present the Christ-event and the revelation through the Christ-event. By constantly actualizing the biblical witness on revelation it renews revelation. It is not enough, e.g., for men to read or hear the scriptures. The scriptural witness must be actual-ized and made concrete in the given situation by the Church seeking the proper human word through which revelation may be re-enacted. Christ promised his Church that 'the Holy Spirit ... will bring to your remembrance all that I have said to you' (Jn 14. 26). But the role of the Spirit is not simply to assist the members of the Church to refresh their memories of past events. Under the guidance of the Spirit they can make present, interpret and help others to experience the on-going reality of revelation in Christ.

In a rich variety of ways the Church makes present and 'transmits' revelation. Liturgy, proclamation, the word of scripture, the teaching of bishops, councils and popes, traditions, the writings of the Fathers, creeds and confessions, the work of theologians – all of these serve to bring alive the divine self-revelation through Christ. In these and other ways the event of revelation is communicated and takes place in the lived reality of a human existence. All of God's people share in this work of 'declaring the wonderful deeds of him' who called us 'out of darkness into his marvellous light' (1 Pet 2.9). They may do this not merely through the public liturgy, preaching, etc., but, e.g., through common prayer in a family and that Christian living by which parents transmit revelation to their children. The whole life of the Church can be significant for the proclamation of the 'wonderful deeds' of God.

It goes without saying that Christians who do not belong to the Roman Catholic Church share in the function of communicating divine revelation. The many forms of their living witness serve to re-actualize the event of divine disclosure through Christ. Moreover the communication of revelation is not to be restricted to more or less conscious Christian witness. Non-Christians could play a part here both in their explicitly religious activities and in other ways. Novels and films, e.g., although not intended to convey God's word to us in Christ, could deal in such a way with guilt, grace and love that they serve to actualize the divine self-revelation to a greater or lesser degree. Among non-Christians the Jews have obviously a special role in communicating revelation through their very existence, their worship and the (Old Testament) scriptures which they share in common with us.

As regards the transmission of revelation we can observe a basic similarity to the original, foundational revelation. Just as it was through word and deed that God's self-manifestation took place in the history of Israel and of Christ, so this twofold structure is discernible in the communication of revelation. The sacraments, e.g., which play an important part in the Church's transmission of revelation, consist at the visible, public level of something being said and something being done. Likewise Christians in their daily living actualize revelation by their actions as well as by their words. Moreover, in the transmission of revelation as well as in its original communication it is the word which has a certain primacy. The words of Jesus at the Last Supper defined in advance the meaning of the deed of Calvary. In revelation the word has a richer function than merely that of indicating meaning and supplying intelligibility. It is a salvific call which changes the hearer. 'Do this in remembrance' (Lk 22. 19) was a personal word of address effectively realized in the lives of believers (cf. 2 Cor 4. 10ff.). Thus in the on-going transmission of revelation in the life of the Church it is the word which supplies the elements of meaning and personal call.

Universal Revelation

When in the preceding section the Church was described as the 'place' where revelation is 'transmitted', does this imply that there is no revelation outside the boundaries of visible Christianity? We should perhaps put the same kind of question first about the original communication of revelation. If Christ in the context of Israelite history is *the* revealer of God, does this exclude any other revelation?

In answering this question it may help to begin by pointing out that Christ *alone* is the saviour of the world. 'There is salvation in no one else, for there is no other name under heaven given among men by which we must be saved' (Acts 4. 12). It is only Christ who communicates salvation: 'God gave us eternal life, and this life is in his Son. He who has the Son has life; he who has not the Son has not life' (1 Jn 5. 11f.). According to men's relation to Christ they will stand or fall in the coming judgment (Mk 8. 38). Yet this should be no fearful and threatening fact, for God wishes all to find salvation through his Son (1 Tim 2. 4). Christ is exclusive saviour, but his salvation is for all. The 'mystery' which has been revealed in Christ is that God's salvific will is universal; it extends to Jews and gentiles alike (Eph 3. 5f.; Col 1. 26f.; Rom 16. 25f.).

Christ's function as saviour runs parallel to his function as revealer. He is the 'one mediator between God and men' (1 Tim 2. 5) who alone mediates revelation and salvation. Yet how can we hold that Christ is such an exclusive, universal revealer when obviously this revelation does not reach all? If we insist on the disclosure in Christ as exclusive, we seem to deny to millions of human beings the possibility of experiencing the divine self-revelation. If we admit that God does make himself known to them, how can we then argue that only the Son has made the Father known? A similar problem faces us when we describe the Church as the 'place' where the divine revelation is transmitted. Does Christian faith involve us in holding that outside the Church there is no revelation? If on the other hand God discloses himself to men who have no allegiance to the Christian community, what role is left for the Church in man's encounter with the divine self-revelation?

One solution to this problem runs as follows. When

Christian faith refers to a revelation which occurred at a particular place and time, viz. through Jesus of Nazareth in the context of Israelite history, it is not denying that revelation was possible and actual at other times and places. It asserts that God's revealing activity reached at that point an expression in history and language which Christians acknowledge as definitive and normative.

Such a reply seems true but insufficient. For just as there is only one saviour for all mankind, so there is only one 'true light that enlightens every man'. The light whether explicitly identified or not is Christ. For all men there is an abiding possibility of knowing God from the external works of his creation and in man's own moral conscious-ness. Now Christ is not merely the goal of this creation, but he is himself the agent of creation: 'All things were created through him' as well as 'for him' (Col 1. 16). In knowing God through creation one knows – however dimly – Christ. In the lives of those millions of people who have heard little or nothing of Christ this revelation works itself out in the complex and mysterious history of their religious experience. It is an element in God's gracious dealing with them, even if this is never consciously realized. Perhaps we can find an illuminating hint in the everyday quality of the parables which Jesus taught. In the very ordinary stuff of life the divine power and rule is open for all to recognize. Yet man must be ready to see and to hear, if he is to catch a glimpse of God's majesty and hear a whisper of his voice.

As regards the Church's role it is necessary to insist that the Church is the divinely established place of revelation and has the authentic means by which the divine disclosure is transmitted in all its fullness. At the same time the Church is more than merely the normative place where revelation is renewed and transmitted. However mysteriously, it is involved wherever the divine revelation becomes an actuality for individual men. The saving call of God which these men hear is in fact – even if never or at best only dimly realized – a gracious invitation that ideally should lead them to become one with the people of God who have been called 'out of darkness' into God's marvellous light.

Disagreement over Revelation

There is a particularly painful problem thrown up by the assertions that the Church is the 'place' of revelation and that all the people of God share in the work of declaring this revelation. What can we make of the scandalous fact that they do not agree in their proclamation? Isn't any claim that the Christian faith is a response to the gracious self-revelation of God ruled out by the widespread, bewildering disagreement among Christians themselves? It may be granted that divine revelation and human faith together make up a living reality, an event which takes place. But this person-to-person encounter does not remain locked up in silent subjectivity; the faith of encounter seeks always to articulate itself in formulations of faith. The problem is that Christians do not agree in these doctrinal statements or 'articles' of faith. Doesn't this failure to agree cast serious doubt on the claim to the experience which is supposed to lie behind these statements, viz. the personal meeting with God? If all Christians have the same experience, surely they would show a far greater degree of agreement in their account of what has taken place? Their dissensions seem to discredit their claim to know God in his self-revelation.

Any reply to this problem must begin with an honest

admission of the scandal of diversity. At the same time, however, it is clear that the ecumenical movement has brought home to many Christians that their doctrinal differences to some extent at least have been verbal and due to a failure to understand what Christians of other traditions were saying. All accounts of revelation are going to be partial, inadequate and in need of qualification. Christians have come more and more to a salutary humility which admits that their doctrinal expressions may not be so comprehensive as once imagined. What was earlier thought to stand in contradiction may now be seen to be concerned with differing aspects of the divine self-revelation.

Yet we should not cheat. We cannot explain away in this fashion all the important differences between the statements which Christians use to interpret the experience of their encounter in Christ with God. We are finally left with some measure of painful disagreement. But after all this is as it were the 'price' which God has to pay for the 'weakness' of his self-manifestation. God does not present himself with irresistible clarity. Room is left for human failure to understand and express what has taken place and does take place in revelation. The divine self-disclosure may not find appropriate human expression because man – wilfully or unwilfully – fails to appreciate what God is saying to him in Christ. We have already noted how faith means primarily the personal relationship of obedient self-commitment and only secondarily statements of faith, viz. doctrines that express the living encounter with God. Now if faith in the primary sense lives only by overcoming the abiding challenge of the 'weakness' of God in his revelation, we can expect a similar problem on the secondary level of doctrinal expression. Here the believing interpretation of man's encounter with God will always be characterized by obscurity, diversity and inadequacy. Overwhelming clarity in the divine revelation would have brought agreement. But God has not chosen to manifest himself unambiguously and irresistibly. The full, open revelation is still to come.

CHAPTER 8

SCRIPTURE, TRADITION AND PROMISE

This last chapter is concerned with two topics, viz. a long-standing problem and a particular, contemporary theology of revelation. The problem is the relation between revelation, scripture and tradition. The theology of revelation is that of Jürgen Moltmann and others who understand revelation in terms of promise.

Scripture and Tradition

The attempt to understand the relation beween scripture, tradition and revelation has given rise to such questions as: (1) Is the whole of revelation contained in scripture alone? (2) Or is it partly contained in tradition? (3) Is it contained wholly both in scripture and tradition? If an affirmative answer is given to (1), theologians would then want to describe scripture as 'sufficient'.

What has been said earlier should make us somewhat dissatisfied with the terms in which these questions are phrased. Revelation is best understood neither as a set of divinely guaranteed truths nor as the communication of these truths, but as a personal event, viz. the saving self-revelation in Jesus of Nazareth by which man is effectively called to enter by faith into a new relationship with God. In these terms it is inappropriate to speak of revelation being 'contained' – either partially or wholly – in scripture. If revelation did consist primarily in 'things', viz. a body of doctrines, we might reasonably retain this kind of talk.

Revelation is, however, a living reality, a personal meeting in man's history which is not happily described as being 'contained' in anything, whether it be scripture or tradition. Likewise it is neither scripture nor tradition but the divine reality alone which we encounter in Christ that is properly speaking 'sufficient'.

How then should we think and talk about the relationship between revelation, scripture and tradition? The difference between revelation and scripture is the difference between a reality and a record. In the past this difference between revelation and scripture was sometimes obscured to the extent that revelation was simply identified with the written word of scripture. The bible and its total content was then understood to be revelation. In fact revelation is both prior to and distinguished from the scriptures. What the scriptures record is not merely the divine revelation itself, but also man's response to it in prayer, liturgy, law, etc. Thus the psalms, the wisdom literature and the historical and prophetical books fill out for us in various ways Old Testament man's reaction to the personal relationship offered him in the divine self-manifestation. The books of the New Testament are recognized by the Church as forming the normative account of the definitive revelation in Christ. Here we have the official record of that apostolic preaching which founded the Church, a preaching which not merely transmitted the foundational revelation that closed with the withdrawal of the risen Lord's visible presence, but which also reflected the fuller understanding that came to the apostles under the guidance of the Holy Spirit. The written apostolic witness remains as something distinct from the original foundational revelation and from that continuing, dependent revelation which began when Peter stood up with the eleven and proclaimed the crucified and risen Lord. The New Testament record functions as the account to which the present, living experience of revelation must be referred. The encounter experienced now is checked against the record written then, and this check takes place in the context of the Church. We read the scriptures as members of a community who enjoy the revelation recorded there and as those who look back to the composition of that record through all the history and tradition of the community.

What then of the relation between revelation and the community tradition? Whether understood as the action of handing on (*traditio*) or as the 'thing' or doctrine handed on (*traditum*), tradition seems best described as the community's traditional interpretation of the revelation recorded in scripture. As such, tradition cannot literally 'hand on' revelation. It is assumed here that we agree that revelation should primarily be seen as that saving call in Christ which man experiences and acknowledges in faith. This living experience cannot be 'handed on' in any ordinary sense. What is properly speaking transmitted and communicated, however, is an account and understanding of this experience. Through tradition we come in contact with a common appreciation transmitted through history, and are enabled to reach a fuller understanding of what we ourselves experience. Tradition means that we can interpret our personal encounter with the self-revealing God not merely through our contemporaries in the believing community but through our predecessors. All of God's people both present and past – whether the entire people of God, bishops, popes, councils, theologians, etc. – share in this work of speaking to us with various degrees of clarity, helpfulness and authority of that revelation which God grants us in his Son. In short revelation can be distinguished from tradition as a living event is to be distinguished from a community understanding transmitted through history.

Revelation and Promise

Up to this point we have been considering revelation in a fragmentary fashion, discussing revelation and faith, revelation and salvation, the close of foundational revelation, etc. But it is hardly enough to explore revelation from various points of view and disown all attempt to synthesize. There are, of course, many theologies of revelation which aim at giving us such a synthesis. To cite some important examples. Revelation may be understood primarily as word (e.g. – with important differences – Bultmann, Barth and Ratzinger), as event (e.g. Pannenberg) or as word and event (e.g. Schillebeeckx and Cullmann). As space does not allow a discussion of the advantages of these various systematic views of revelation, we can deal only with one, viz. the attempt to understand the structure of revelation in terms of promise. Such a theology of revelation is found in the writings of J.B. Metz (Münster), Jürgen Moltmann (Tübingen) and Gerhard Sauter (Göttingen). Without necessarily adopting precisely the views of any of these three writers we can sketch out an approach to revelation as conveyed by the divine promise which calls human hope to life.

This theology of revelation refuses to begin from the view that revelation is the disclosure of what is concealed or the manifestation of what is hidden. This would be to establish a starting-point by simply formally 'unpacking' the notion of revelation as the removal of the veil (*velum*) and the making clear and visible what had hitherto been unseen, misunderstood or not even guessed at. Scripture, however, would suggest another starting-point, viz. that revelation must be taken as the promise which calls man's hope to life. For God reveals himself by way of promise and in the unfolding history of promise. Thus the history of the Israelites begins when God reveals himself to Abraham in the context of promise: 'Go from your country and your kindred and your father's house to the land that I will show you. And I will make of you a great nation, and I will bless you, and make your name great, so that you will be a blessing' (Gen 12. 1f.). The encounter of Moses with God is likewise a revelation in which God promises to deliver the Israelites from the slavery of Egypt and give them 'a land flowing with milk and honey' (Exod 3. 1ff.). Examples could be multiplied from both Old and New Testaments to establish this point, viz. that God reveals himself in a setting of promise and the fulfilment of promise.

This understanding of revelation implies the notions of (1) divine election, covenant and sending and (2) human hope and obedience. God calls to hope the people whom he has chosen as his own. In his covenant-promise, whether to Abraham, on Mt Sinai or at the death and resurrection of Christ, God not merely binds himself to be faithful but also summons man to a future. He calls to a mission and summons into the history of promise those who enter the covenant with him. On man's side this means not only a believing hope aroused by the divine promise but also an active obedience. The Epistle to the Hebrews draws together the notions of human obedience and that divine revelation which invites man into an unfolding history of promise. Abraham not merely believes and hopes in the promise but obeys it: 'By faith Abraham obeyed when he was called to go out to a place which he was to receive as an inheritance; and he went out, not knowing where he was to go. By faith

78

he sojourned in the land of promise, as in a foreign land, living in tents with Isaac and Jacob, heirs with him of the same promise' (11. 8f.). What was to come was more valuable, more real to Abraham than the present or the past. The invisible future reality had full authority over him.

If we understand revelation basically as promise this will affect the structure of our thinking about God so that the continuing fidelity of God will assume central importance. Our knowledge of God is no *résumé* of static 'facts' but a knowledge of what he will be, viz. the faithful God. He is revealed as the one who calls, promises and 'keeps faith for ever' (Ps 146. 6). It is not that man knows God merely as the one who has faithfully fulfilled his promises. Recalling the divine fidelity in history, man reaches forward to the future, trusting in the promised loyalty of God. This is a knowledge which 'anticipates' the future of God, so to speak, as the 'God before us', the God of hope (Rom 15. 13). If the words of Exodus 3. 14 are translated 'I will be what I will be' they suggest the 'futurity' of God which shapes our understanding of him. We do not as it were 'have' God but we await him in a hope called to life by his promise.

If revelation is described as promise and man appropriates the divine promise in believing hope, what is the 'content' of this promise? What is it that man comes to expect? Essentially it is something new. God's self-revealing promise is not primarily the disclosure of what is now present but hidden; nor is it the manifestation of something which took place in the past and the meaning of which has so far eluded us. The revelation in which Abraham was promised that he would enjoy a new land and would be the father of a great people contradicted in fact all the present and past data. For he was called to uproot himself, separate himself from his clan and wander into an unknown situation in which the promise would be fulfilled. Contemporary or previous events, far from suggesting that this fulfilment was likely or even possible, strongly suggested the opposite. Experience argued that this was not the way to produce a great people. A migrant family could normally expect nothing else than that after some time they would be simply absorbed into the foreign people among whom they had come to live. Then Sarah's sterility (Gen 18. 9-15) seemed to make the realization of the promise even more improbable. So far from drawing on anything in present or past experience the divine promise to Abraham stood in conflict with experience as the promise of something quite new. The position was similar with the promise of a new land. Eventually Abraham could call his own merely a small piece of land in Mamre and his tenure of even this property was continually threatened. Quite reasonably he asked: 'O Lord God, how am I to know that I shall possess it?' (Gen 15. 8). In fact Abraham could 'know' this only by trusting that God would be enduringly loyal to his promise and would bring about something new in man's experience.

The revealing promise is not a disclosure or reminder of some meaning which is there in the events we experience but which we have so far not grasped. Nor is the promise concerned with a renewal, a return to something original. The 'new' thing which God will bring is no continuation of or return to the past, but the future will see something which has not yet been. Hence to know God in his self-revealing promise is not simply the result of returning to our origin as creatures of God. The divine revelation is much more than a call to emerge from our forgetfulness and appreciate what we originally were or what we now are: 'It does not yet appear what we shall be' (1 Jn 3. 2).

Now it is true that in the Old Testament the promised

future was described by the prophets on the analogy of God's activity in fulfilling his promises in Israel's past. There was to be a new occupation of the land (Amos), the establishment of a new David and a new Sion (Isaiah), a new exodus (second Isaiah) and a new covenant (Jeremiah). What was promised could well have sounded as if it were to be a renewal, the return to what had once been enjoyed but was later lost. Yet in fact what was to come would break the original patterns. The saving divine revelation would not be confined to the people of Israel, but would include all nations. The promised salvation was not simply this-worldly but was to reach beyond death. Through the prophets God was revealing himself in a promise which was pointing to something truly new. To quote second Isaiah: 'Remember not the former things, nor consider the things of old. Behold, I am doing a new thing' (43. 18f.). The future was not to be the return of an original, 'golden' age. The 'new' thing would not agree happily with what had gone before but would be in conflict – even painful conflict – with what men were accustomed to.

With Christ's death and resurrection came an event that was not merely genuinely new, but also definitively so. The resurrection brought the last age of God's promise, showing once and for all and for all mankind the divine fidelity, viz. that God was faithful to his people in the person of his Son. Yet the resurrection should be understood as revelatory not merely in terms of its being the fulfilment of promise; it must be viewed in the context of our hope for the promised future. To know the resurrection of Christ is to recognize in this event the future of man. The resurrection not merely confirms the divine promises, but opens up a new hope. For God discloses himself as the one who raises and will raise the dead. As regards Christ himself the resurrection reveals not only the meaning of his person, his life and his death, but it points to his future. The 'history' of the risen Christ is still going on. He has a genuine future as the one for whom we wait in hope; he encounters us insofar as he is in movement to the goal. Thus the revelation in Christ is related to a reality not yet there. This is illustrated by the fact that the words of the risen Christ are concerned not merely with self-identification, but with promise and mission. For the first Christians recognizing the revelation brought with the resurrection meant recognizing in the risen Lord their own future and mission. 'Jesus came and said to them, "All authority in heaven and on earth has been given to me. Go therefore and make disciples of all nations ... and lo, I am with you always, to the close of the age" (Mt 28. 18-20).

With this understanding of the resurrection Moltmann can write: 'The centre of the New Testament scriptures is the risen Christ's future, which they announce, show and promise. Hence to understand the biblical writings in their proclamation ... we must look in the same direction as they do' (*Theology of Hope,* 283). What does lie ahead? What is the 'content' of the revealing promise which we find in the resurrection? It is not merely the unveiling of what has already secretly taken place in Christ and is now present needing only to be disclosed. The reality of the risen Lord is not yet closed. The resurrection is an event which opens a process and grounds a hope that points to the future of man and the world in the future of Christ. On his side the lordship of the crucified one over the whole world is coming in a victory that has still to be completed. 'He must reign until he has put all his enemies under his feet. The last enemy to be destroyed is death.' Evil and death must pass. It is only when all things have been subjected to Christ that he will 'deliver the kingdom to God the Father' (1 Cor 15. 20-28).

Such a view of the revelatory value of Christ's resurrection suggests the kind of response we could make to the rejection of the resurrection on the grounds that it offers no comparison to what we experience. It is commonly presupposed that events will show a broadly similar structure, so that alleged happenings may be denied if they show no analogy to what is already known through common experience. By means of repeatedly attested facts we are enabled to assign or deny likelihood to alleged events and to explain what is unknown in one case from what is known in another. It is not uniformity which is being presupposed but a certain common core of resemblance on the basis of which the special features of particular events can be appreciated. As the resurrection shows no analogy, no common core of resemblance to repeatedly attested events, it is to be rejected. Now such a supposition is part of a Greek view of the universe in which there is 'nothing new under the sun' and for which the past is the decisive criterion. What guarantees that the past must enjoy such paramount importance? If we wish to find comparisons in the case of the resurrection, we should look to the future rather than to the past. Christ's resurrection offers an analogy not to what we constantly experience, but to what we hope for.

So much then by way of sketchy outline of a theology of revelation based on promise. What kind of arguments can be brought for and against such a view?

It could seem that with the future enjoying a primacy of importance the role of the past and the present is belittled. In fact for such a view of revelation the past and the present do retain their importance if only in relation to the future. We look back now to the promises of the past to be directed to the future. The events which are recalled – whether they belong to the Old or New Testament – are

recognized to be genuinely revelatory, but only provision-
ally so. The events of the exodus, e.g., no less than those of
Christ's death and resurrection direct us back to the
future, so that from coming history we await not only the
future of the present but also the future of the past. In this
view the past is a promise of the future; recollection is a
mode of hope. In its revealing and saving significance we
celebrate the Eucharist as promise, proclaiming (in the
present) the Lord's death (in the past) *until he comes*
(1 Cor 11. 26).

In Chapter 1 we considered the correlative functions of
word and event in the structure of divine revelation. Does
the kind of theology of revelation we have just outlined
require that we must go back on all that? No. It means
rather that God's word to man is to be understood
primarily as a word of promise and the events as events of
promise. God has revealed himself in man's history
through word and event, in that at particular times,
through particular events and to a definite group of people
his promise came. There is no need either to withdraw the
description of revelation as a saving call in Christ to enter
by faith into a personal relationship with God. This call is
now to be specified as a call by way of promise to which
man responds in faith and hope.

A more troublesome criticism is that a theology of
revelation in terms of promise is selective in its use of
scripture. Those biblical elements which either do not fit
into the scheme or would fit only with difficulty are left out.
Thus the Epistle to the Hebrews with its stress on the
future is highlighted in Moltmann's *Theology of Hope* but
there is not a single reference to St John's Gospel. An
answer can be suggested in terms of a word which has been
so far avoided in this book, viz. eschatology, i.e. the
doctrine of the last age and final destiny both of individuals

and of mankind in general. In the fourth Gospel the stress is on realized eschatology, i.e. on what has been achieved and is now present. 'He who believes in the Son has eternal life' (3. 36); 'he who does not believe is condemned already' (3. 18). On the other hand the Epistle to the Hebrews puts the emphasis on what is still to come: 'Christ will appear a second time ... to save those who are eagerly waiting for him' (9. 28). The New Testament simply does not present us with a uniform view of eschatology. Both in this respect and in general the scriptures, being greater than any theological system, cannot finally be brought into a single synthesis. The kind of evidence introduced above suggests that there is an arguable case for seizing on promise as the central biblical theme and understanding revelation primarily as a divine promise which calls to life man's believing hope.

But does such a theology present us with a cheap hope which fails to take suffering seriously and ignores the scandal of the cross? In reply it could be urged that far from treating suffering lightly this theology of revelation in a sense accentuates it. It is precisely in hoping for what is to come that the believer experiences the pain of the present. He recognizes the deep difference between the reality under which he suffers and the reality he awaits.

In favour of the view of revelation as promise we can note how it means a firm stress on the collective element in Christianity. As the divine promise is a promise to all, the future is a future common to all; we should live inspired by our common hope. Such an emphasis on the future almost inevitably means a greater social consciousness. It is no accident that the Epistle to the Hebrews with its characteristic stress on future eschatology develops the theme of Christians as the new pilgrim people of God. True hope leads our thinking away from individualism.

With this appreciation of the future and the collective goes a conviction that the believing hope called into being by the divine promise is essentially active. The expectation of our future does not leave us to endure present evil with passive patience, but provides the consistent impulse towards the realization of justice, freedom and full humanity precisely in the light of the future which has been announced to us. God's revealing promise calls for our creative, militant and responsible action. It should not leave Christians in the state of a passive, gloomy resignation which lacks the will to change.

It is easy to see how the theology of revelation we have considered readily yields a Christian ethic. The command-ments are the ethical side of the revelation through promise. Like the promise they are not abstract, timeless norms, but have a future-directedness, aiming at that reality of human dignity by which man might become worthy of intimate communion with the God of hope. In other words this means taking as the basis of our ethical thinking the prayer, 'that we may be made worthy of the promises of Christ'. The hope which grasps the divine promise is a responsible, obedient hope, performing now in expectation of Christ's coming whatever makes straight the way of the Lord. Christian ethics are determined then not by a fixed natural order but by the God of the future who promises, 'Behold, I make all things new'. To be truly a man is to live out this hope based on the divine promise.

There are other arguments both against and for such a theology of revelation in terms of promise. We can conclude with one last point in favour of the view put forward by Moltmann, Metz and Sauter. Christians must be ready for the genuinely new. So often they fear what is new, judge it wholly in terms of the present situation or will accept it only if it can be shown to be merely a 're-newal', a return, e.g., to something in primitive Christianity. This desire to return to the past or to see the past return can mean that the claim of the future – conveyed by the very promises given in the past – may not be heard. Such a fear of the new is not a Christian attitude. What is called for is a venture forward into the future in which we are drawn on in hope by the God who reveals himself to us in the unfolding history of his promise.

CHAPTER 9

CONCLUSION

In writing a study on the way in which God has revealed himself to man it is uncomfortably obvious that such theologizing can appear divorced from reality, whereas it should always be an expression of faith and an aid to Christian preaching. For those who feel that they have never known the Father of Our Lord Jesus Christ may this book have helped to give them a glimpse of something that has so far eluded their experience. For those who have been conscious of the gracious presence of God in Christ may this book – far from dulling that reality for them – have clarified their experience and aroused a greater longing for that encounter with the self-revealing God. Theology – above all a study of God's revelation in Christ – should not leave us at the level of disinterested, quasi-scientific abstraction, but should lead us to or back to the area of personal concern, where we may express ourselves in the confession of faith and the prayer of hope. Come, Lord Jesus.

EXTRACT FROM THE DOGMATIC CONSTITUTION ON DIVINE REVELATION OF VATICAN II

Preface

1 Hearing the word of God with reverence and proclaiming it confidently, this most sacred Synod takes its direction from these words of St John: 'We announce to you the eternal life which was with the Father, and has appeared to us. What we have seen and have heard we announce to you, in order that you also may have fellowship with us, and that our fellowship may be with the Father, and with his Son Jesus Christ' (1 Jn 1. 2-3). Therefore, following in the footsteps of the Councils of Trent and of First Vatican, this present Council wishes to set forth authentic teaching about divine revelation and about how it is handed on, so that by hearing the message of salvation the whole world may believe; by believing, it may hope; and by hoping, it may love.

Chapter 1: Revelation Itself

2 In his goodness and wisdom, God chose to reveal himself and to make known to us the hidden purpose of his will (cf. Eph 1. 9) by which through Christ, the Word made flesh, man has access to the Father in the Holy Spirit and comes to share in the divine nature (cf. Eph 2. 18; 2 Pet 1. 4). Through this revelation, therefore, the invisible God (cf. Col 1. 15; 1 Tim 1. 17) out of the abundance of his love speaks to men as friends (cf. Exod 33. 11; Jn 15. 14-15)

and lives among them (cf. Bar 3. 38), so that he may invite and take them into fellowship with himself. This plan of revelation is realized by deeds and words having an inner unity; the deeds wrought by God in the history of salvation manifest and confirm the teaching and realities signified by the words, while the words proclaim the deeds and clarify the mystery contained in them. By this revelation then, the deepest truth about God and the salvation of man is made clear to us in Christ, who is the Mediator and at the same time the fullness of all revelation.

3 God, who through the Word creates all things (cf. Jn 1. 3) and keeps them in existence, gives men an enduring witness to himself in created realities (cf. Rom 1. 19-20). Planning to make known the way of heavenly salvation, he went further and from the start manifested himself to our first parents. Then after their fall his promise of redemption aroused in them the hope of being saved (cf. Gen 3. 15), and from that time on he ceaselessly kept the human race in his care, in order to give eternal life to those who perseveringly do good in search of salvation (cf. Rom 2. 6-7). Then, at the time he had appointed, he called Abraham in order to make of him a great nation (cf. Gen 12. 2). Through the patriarchs, and after them through Moses and the prophets, he taught this nation to acknowledge himself as the one living and true God, provident Father and just Judge, and to wait for the Saviour promised by him. In this manner he prepared the way for the gospel down through the centuries.

4 Then, after speaking in many places and varied ways through the prophets, God 'last of all in these days has spoken to us by his Son' (Heb 1. 1-2). For he sent his Son, the eternal Word, who enlightens all men, so that he might

dwell among men and tell them the innermost realities about God (cf. Jn 1. 1-18). Jesus Christ, therefore, the Word made flesh, sent as 'a man to men', 'speaks the words of God' (Jn 3. 34), and completes the work of salvation which his Father gave him to do (cf. Jn 5. 36; 17. 4). To see Jesus is to see his Father (Jn 14. 9). For this reason Jesus perfected revelation by fulfilling it through his whole work of making himself present and manifesting himself: through his words and deeds, his signs and wonders but especially through his death and glorious resurrection from the dead and final sending of the Spirit of truth. Moreover, he confirmed with divine testimony what revelation proclaimed: that God is with us to free us from the darkness of sin and death, and to raise us up to life eternal.

The Christian dispensation, therefore, as the new and definitive covenant, will never pass away, and we now await no further new public revelation before the glorious manifestation of our Lord Jesus Christ (cf. 1 Tim 6. 14 and Tit 2. 13).

5 'The obedience of faith' (Rom 16. 26; cf. 1. 5; 2 Cor 10. 5-6) must be given to God who reveals, an obedience by which man entrusts his whole self freely to God, offering 'the full submission of intellect and will to God who reveals', and freely assenting to the truth revealed by him. If this faith is to be shown, the grace of God and the interior help of the Holy Spirit must precede and assist, moving the heart and turning it to God, opening the eyes of the mind, and giving 'joy and ease to everyone in assenting to the truth and believing it'. To bring about an ever deeper understanding of revelation, the same Holy Spirit constantly brings faith to completion by his gifts.

6 Through divine revelation, God chose to show forth and communicate himself and the eternal decisions of his will regarding the salvation of men. That is to say, he chose 'to share those divine treasures which totally transcend the understanding of the human mind' (First Vatican Council. Dz 3005).

This sacred Synod affirms, 'God, the beginning and end of all things, can be known with certainty from created reality by the light of human reason' (cf. Rom 1. 20); but the Synod teaches that it is through his revelation 'that those religious truths which are by their nature accessible to human reason can be known by all men with ease, with solid certitude, and with no trace of error, even in the present state of the human race' (First Vatican Council. Dz 3004-5).

(Translation from *The Documents of Vatican II*, ed. Walter M. Abbott, S.J., Geoffrey Chapman, London-Dublin, 1966.)

INDEX

Barr, James: *Old and New in Interpretation* (London, 1966); discusses helpfully such issues as revelation through history and the link between revelation and salvation.

Benoît, P., O.P.; *Inspiration and the Bible* (English trans., London, 1965, p.b.); even if more concerned with inspiration and the doctrine of St Thomas, does summarize well some of the biblical data concerning revelation.

Fries, H.: 'Offenbarung', *Mysterium Salutis*, vol. 1, 159-238, ed. J. Feiner and M. Löhrer (Einsiedeln, 1965); the most satisfying account of revelation by a Roman Catholic. This volume, which is being translated into English, contains relevant and valuable essays by other authors on such subjects as salvation history, scripture and tradition, faith and the transmission of revelation in the Church.

Latourelle, R., S.J. *The Theology of Revelation* (English trans., New York, 1966); this and Moran's book (see below) are the best works on revelation by Roman Catholic authors now available in English.

Metz, J.B.: 'The Church and the World', *The Word in History*, 69-85, ed. T.P. Burke (New York, 1966).

Moltmann, J.: *Theology of Hope* (English trans., London, 1967). Like Metz Moltmann gives us an understanding of revelation that is thoroughly eschatological; see ch. 8 above.

Moran, G.: *Theology of Revelation* (New York, 1966; London, 1967).

Niebuhr, H.R.: *The Meaning of Revelation* (New York, 1960, p.b.); a graceful study of revelation which stresses personal values without belittling the place of the historical community.

Ratzinger, J. and Rahner, K.: *Revelation and Tradition* (English trans. Freiburg, 1966); both authors emphasize how revelation exists only where it calls forth faith. Ratzinger discusses well the relations of revelation, scripture and tradition.

Schutz, R. and Thurian, M: *La Parole vivante au Concile* (2 ed. Taizé, 1966); a valuable guide to the teaching of Vatican II on revelation.

Wilckens, U.: *God's Revelation* (English trans., London, 1967, p.b.); a careful study of the New Testament data. Wilckens is a fine New Testament scholar, perhaps the most valuable theologian in the Pannenberg circle.